The Promise of the New and Genealogies of Education Reform

This volume explores questions about hope, optimism and the possibilities of the 'new' as expressed in educational thinking on the nature and problem of adolescence. One focus is on the interwar years in Australian education, and the proliferation of educational reports and programs directed to understanding, governing, educating and enlivening adolescents. This included studies of the secondary school curriculum, reviews of teaching of civics and democracy, the development of guidance programs, the specification of the needs and attributes of the adolescent, and interventions to engage the 'average student' in post-primary schooling. Framed by imperatives to respond in new ways to educational problems, and to the call of modernity, many of these programs and reforms conveyed a sense of enormous optimism in the compelling power of education and schools to foster new personal and social knowledge and transformation. A second focus is the expression of such utopianism in educational history – themes that may seem novel, or incongruous, or even inexplicable in the present – and in studies and representations of young people as citizens in the making. Finally, developing broadly genealogical approaches to the study of adolescence, the chapters variously seek to provoke more explicitly historical thinking about the construction of the field of youth studies.

This book was originally published as a special issue of the *Journal of Educational Administration and History*.

Julie McLeod is a Professor, Graduate School of Education, at the University of Melbourne, Australia, an Australian Research Council Future Fellow, and an Editor of the journal *Gender and Education*. Her research and publications are in the sociology and history of education, with a focus on gender, youth identity, curriculum, inequality and social change.

Katie Wright is an Australian Research Council Fellow (DECRA) in the Graduate School of Education at the University of Melbourne, Australia. Her research interests focus on historical and sociological studies of psychology, education and childhood. Recent publications include *The Rise of the Therapeutic Society: Psychological Knowledge & the Contradictions of Cultural Change* (New Academia, 2011).

The Promise of the New and Genealogies of Education Reform

Edited by
Julie McLeod and Katie Wright

LONDON AND NEW YORK

First published 2015 by Routledge

2 Park Square, Milton Park, Abingdon, Oxfordshire OX14 4RN
711 Third Avenue, New York, NY 10017

Routledge is an imprint of the Taylor & Francis Group, an informa business

First issued in paperback 2018

Copyright © 2015 Taylor & Francis

All rights reserved. No part of this book may be reprinted or reproduced or utilised in any form or by any electronic, mechanical, or other means, now known or hereafter invented, including photocopying and recording, or in any information storage or retrieval system, without permission in writing from the publishers.

Notice:
Product or corporate names may be trademarks or registered trademarks, and are used only for identification and explanation without intent to infringe.

British Library Cataloguing in Publication Data
A catalogue record for this book is available from the British Library

ISBN 13: 978-1-138-80775-4 (hbk)
ISBN 13: 978-1-138-37945-9 (pbk)

Typeset in Times New Roman
by RefineCatch Limited, Bungay, Suffolk

Publisher's Note
The publisher accepts responsibility for any inconsistencies that may have arisen during the conversion of this book from journal articles to book chapters, namely the possible inclusion of journal terminology.

Disclaimer
Every effort has been made to contact copyright holders for their permission to reprint material in this book. The publishers would be grateful to hear from any copyright holder who is not here acknowledged and will undertake to rectify any errors or omissions in future editions of this book.

Contents

Citation Information	vii
Notes on Contributors	ix
1. The promise of the new: genealogies of youth, nation and educational reform in Australia *Julie McLeod and Katie Wright*	1
2. 'Pupils differently circumstanced and with other aims': governing the post-primary child in early twentieth-century Australia *Phil Cormack*	13
3. 'To see through Johnny and to see Johnny through': the guidance movement in interwar Australia *Katie Wright*	35
4. Educating for 'world-mindedness': cosmopolitanism, localism and schooling the adolescent citizen in interwar Australia *Julie McLeod*	57
5. A new teacher for a new nation? Teacher education, 'English', and schooling in early twentieth-century Australia *Bill Green and Jo-Anne Reid*	79
6. Reflections: continuing the conversation *Maxine Stephenson*	99
Index	109

Citation Information

The chapters in this book were originally published in the *Journal of Educational Administration and History*, volume 44, issue 4 (November 2012). When citing this material, please use the original page numbering for each article, as follows:

Chapter 1
The promise of the new: genealogies of youth, nation and educational reform in Australia
Julie McLeod and Katie Wright
Journal of Educational Administration and History, volume 44, issue 4 (November 2012) pp. 283–294

Chapter 2
'Pupils differently circumstanced and with other aims': governing the post-primary child in early twentieth-century Australia
Phil Cormack
Journal of Educational Administration and History, volume 44, issue 4 (November 2012) pp. 295–316

Chapter 3
'To see through Johnny and to see Johnny through': the guidance movement in interwar Australia
Katie Wright
Journal of Educational Administration and History, volume 44, issue 4 (November 2012) pp. 317–338

Chapter 4
Educating for 'world-mindedness': cosmopolitanism, localism and schooling the adolescent citizen in interwar Australia
Julie McLeod
Journal of Educational Administration and History, volume 44, issue 4 (November 2012) pp. 339–360

Chapter 5
A new teacher for a new nation? Teacher education, 'English', and schooling in early twentieth-century Australia
Bill Green and Jo-Anne Reid
Journal of Educational Administration and History, volume 44, issue 4 (November 2012) pp. 361–380

CITATION INFORMATION

Chapter 6
Reflections: continuing the conversation
Maxine Stephenson
Journal of Educational Administration and History, volume 44, issue 4 (November 2012) pp. 381–390

Please direct any queries you may have about the citations to clsuk.permissions@cengage.com

Notes on Contributors

Phil Cormack is Adjunct Research Associate Professor in the School of Education at the University of South Australia, Australia. His areas of research interest include education of adolescents, history of education, literacy and language education and critical discourse analysis. He has published extensively in these areas and worked across policy, school and academic domains.

Bill Green is Emeritus Professor, School of Teacher Education, Charles Sturt University, New South Wales, Australia. His research interests are in curriculum inquiry and literacy studies, curriculum history, doctoral research education, professional practice and education, and education for rural-regional sustainability. His recent publications include the co-edited volumes *Literacy in 3D: An Integrated Perspective in Theory and Practice* (2012), *Rethinking Rural Literacies: Transnational Perspectives* (2013), and *Body/Practice: The Body in Professional Practice, Learning and Education* (2014).

Julie McLeod is Professor, Graduate School of Education, University of Melbourne, Australia, an Australian Research Council Future Fellow (2012–2016), and an Editor of the journal *Gender and Education*. Her research is in the history and sociology of education: current projects include a genealogy of adolescence and citizenship education; a history of school design and pedagogical innovation, and a study on youth identity and social science expertise. Recent publications include *Researching Social Change: Qualitative Approaches* (with R. Thomson, 2009); *Making Modern Lives: Subjectivity, Schooling and Social Change* (with L. Yates, 2006).

Jo-Anne Reid is Professor of Education in the Faculty of Education, Charles Sturt University, New South Wales, Australia. Her research projects have focused on English teaching, teacher education (including overseas-born and -educated non-native English-speaking teachers and the career pathways of Indigenous teachers), literacy and the environment, and rural teacher education. She has published widely on classroom practice and research, both alone and in collaboration with others.

Maxine Stephenson is Senior Lecturer at The University of Auckland's Faculty of Education, Auckland, New Zealand. She teaches History and Sociology of Education in the School of Critical Studies in Education. She has been both a secondary school educator and an early childhood educator.

Katie Wright is an Australian Research Council Fellow (DECRA) at the University of Melbourne, Australia. Her major research interests concern the role and effects of psychological knowledges and therapeutic discourses in social change, cultural life and educational contexts. Current research projects include a study of public inquiries into childhood maltreatment, a genealogical study of adolescence and schooling, and an investigation of contemporary and historical understandings of youth mental health and wellbeing. Recent publications include *The Rise of the Therapeutic Society: Psychological Knowledge & the Contradictions of Cultural Change* (New Academia, 2011).

The promise of the new: genealogies of youth, nation and educational reform in Australia

Julie McLeod and Katie Wright

Melbourne Graduate School of Education, The University of Melbourne, Melbourne, Australia

> The promise of the new underpins much educational reform discourse, from utopian strands and grand gestures to more formulaic rhetoric found in declarations of new policies for new times. Informed by genealogical and feminist approaches, this essay introduces some conceptual frameworks for analysing such expressions of hopefulness and newness in educational discourse. While its initial impetus is debates about the education of adolescents in interwar Australia, it extends to a consideration of relations between future-oriented utopian aspirations in the past and educational discourses and practices in the present. It calls for more reflexive problematisation of the past–present relationship in historical and sociological studies of education, and outlines an argument for taking account of the 'untimely' in educational discourses and practices. The essay concludes with an overview of the articles featured in this volume.

Introduction

This special issue of the *Journal of Educational Administration and History* addresses questions about hope, optimism and possibilities for transformation, as expressed in educational thinking on adolescence, citizenship and the nation. Developing broadly genealogical approaches, the articles explore in various ways 'the promise of the new' in educational history and also seek to provoke more explicitly historical thinking about contemporary educational reform. The focus is discussions in Australian education in the early decades of the twentieth century, although the issues raised resonate beyond these national and temporal borders. The call of the 'new' underpins much educational reform discourse, from utopian strands and grand gestures to the more formulaic rhetoric found in declarations of new policies for new times. In the present, it is perhaps easy to become indifferent to the repeated claims to newness or alternatively to regard the confident optimism of earlier times or hopes for radical change as hopelessly innocent and misguided. Yet there is value, as the essays here suggest, in pausing and trying to look again at the promise of the new, to better understand the reforms being ushered in and the types of problems they both constructed and responded to. This also invites, we propose, reflection on the ways in which contemporary educational reforms are imagined and agendas for change discursively represented.

An initial impetus to the special issue focus on youth, citizen and nation was the proliferation during the early decades and interwar years of the twentieth century of educational reports and programmes directed towards understanding and educating adolescents in secondary school settings. These included studies of the secondary school curriculum, reviews of teaching civics and democracy, the development of psychological and vocational guidance programmes, specification of the needs and attributes of the adolescent, interventions to engage the 'average student' in post-primary schooling, and the role, preparation and conduct of good teachers who would be able to engage the new pupil. These wide-ranging deliberations regarding the purposes of schooling and the pressing need for educational reform expressed an enthusiasm for the possibilities afforded by modern educational approaches. Capturing this mood and a self-conscious awareness of the dawn of new times, Percival Cole (1935) of the Teachers' College, Sydney, writing in his edited volume, *The education of the adolescent in Australia*, reflected that: 'But the greatest transition of all is gradually being made, from an old view of life to a new view of life, from an old educational theory to a new educational theory, from old types of school to new types of school' (p. xi).

Framed by the call of modernity and imperatives to respond to the 'new', many of the programmes and reforms of this era conveyed a sense of enormous confidence in the compelling power of schools to foster new personal and social knowledge and transformation, and to open new opportunities for the regulation and education of adolescents. Such expressions of hope and the allure of new ideas and approaches constitute the second focus of this special issue. Noting the pervasiveness of these ideas at the beginning of the twentieth century, Brehony (2000) observes that 'the adjective "new" was very much in vogue, especially when used in tandem with nouns such as "woman", "psychology" and "education"' (p. 115). We are interested, then, in what the seemingly perennial fascination with the 'new' in educational policy amounts to, how it manifests in different times and places, and with what effects.

We begin this opening essay with some brief reflections on utopianism in education, historically and in the present, before offering some comments on the value of genealogical approaches for exploring these matters and for fostering a critical interrogation of past–present relations in the history of education and in the history of the educational present. The final section maps the key themes and arguments addressed in the articles that follow.

Optimism, utopianism and the perpetual search for the 'new'

During the early decades of the twentieth century, the tremendous sense of optimism about the transformative power of education gave schooling a critical role in advancing the economic and social progress of the newly federated Australian nation. Leading educationalists looked abroad for new ideas that might be drawn upon to inform local approaches. Many undertook study tours of the USA, Britain and Continental Europe, and the investigations of educational practices elsewhere inspired visions for change. The areas of interest traversed the gamut of educational issues – from the purposes of schooling and educational administration to explorations of new kinds of knowledges about pedagogy and the developing child. The search for ideas that might inform the development of improved approaches was particularly urgent in the context of an expanding school system.

Understood within the broader social context of the early twentieth century, the search for new educational ideas and practices and the enthusiasm for modern approaches to schooling were perhaps in some ways unremarkable, reflecting the spirit of the times. Yet, looked at from a comparative historical perspective, they highlight the very different ways in which educational aspirations for the future are articulated in the present. What might particular moments of optimism in the past suggest in relation to understanding present-day educational trajectories and reform agendas? In Australia, these agendas include, amongst other things, the introduction of national high-stakes testing through NAPLAN (National Assessment Program – Literacy and Numeracy), the development of the Australian Curriculum and recent approaches to the promotion of student wellbeing and 'positive education'. We would suggest that such new initiatives and reforms in the current era are not heralded in with the same kinds of expansive and transformative potential that characterised the reforms from the early twentieth century. This is not to say that current programmes are not future-oriented or do not have a powerful change agenda; they most certainly do, as critics of neo-liberalism and marketisation in education have so thoroughly documented.

Yet, in important respects, discourses of educational change today seem rather mixed and fragmented, indeed more muted. On the one hand, every school and educational agency has a vision, a mission statement that is forward-thinking, goal-oriented and client-focused. On the other hand, this is probably heard more as policy compliance, rather than as educational innovation. In the language of neo-liberalism, reforms are more likely to be couched in terms of claims for greater efficiency, accountability and transparency than in the possibility of radical overhaul (though, of course, some proponents of the efficiency agenda would likely see this as a major overhaul). There is perhaps a jaded and even sceptical sense of what the new can actually offer, whether the new is possible or if it can only be repackaged, borrowed or recycled. Moreover, the repetitiveness to claims of the new can dull an appreciation of times when ideas and reforms were indeed new and startling, and it can work against exploring how notions of the new and educational reform are mobilised differently in the present. Of course, the social, political and economic contexts, both locally and globally, are radically different now from the early twentieth century. Nevertheless, the enthusiasm and optimism expressed in educational discourses in those earlier times are striking. They provide, we propose, an important counterpoint for thinking afresh about the kinds of educational policy aspirations that are prevalent today and the types of visions for the future that might emerge in looking back as well as forward.

There is a long thread of utopian thought in education, and it has moved in and out of critical favour, with Webb (2009, p. 743) noting that a few decades ago, 'utopia seemed moribund'. More recently, there has been a renewal of critical interest in utopian thinking in education and Webb (2009, p. 744) suggests that utopianism is 'slowly emerging from the shadows and losing its pejorative connotations'. He argues that the current era of managerialism and marketisation has prompted growing recognition of the need for alternative visions in education; moreover, he suggests that what is needed is a kind of 'good' utopianism grounded in practical possibilities, in contrast to a 'bad' utopianism that in Webb's (2009) view is either too unrealistic or too doctrinaire (p. 745). Halpin (2003) has similarly argued that education today is in need of new utopian visions. For Halpin, the state of being hopeful about the future entails a critical attitude towards the present: it 'implicitly involves a critical reflective attitude towards prevailing circumstances'. As such, it also reflects discontent, 'inasmuch as a person's hopes for the future may make them very dissatisfied with things as they are presently' (Halpin 2003, p. 15). Utopianism is, in Halpin's view, about recognition of the limitations or deficiencies of the present and the will to change things for the better.

Perhaps the most important aspect of utopianism for our present discussion, at least as we are employing this concept in relation to a future-oriented hopefulness about educational change (Halpin 2003), is that it points to the complexity of educational change and works against simplified views that are either overly optimistic or pessimistic. On the one hand, some sceptics might see utopianism as excessively – and even dangerously – optimistic and romantic; on the other hand, some currents of Foucauldian and poststructural theorising can implicitly posit a pessimistic account of the possibilities for change, focusing on regulation, governance and normativity. Our interest here is in bringing together explorations of hope and utopianism with Foucauldian approaches, to consider how this intersection might offer ways out of unhelpful binary constructions of educational reform.

Genealogy, history and educational reform

Thinking about hope, optimism and the utopian aspirations of education brings issues of temporality into sharp relief. Educational practices and systems are rarely static, and it is a common trope in the history of education for the period under study to be identified as one of change. Discourses of educational change also implicitly or explicitly privilege new and better ways of doing things. As such, they are, naturally, future-oriented. But our interest here is also in looking back, in productive terms, as understood by Foucault. And it is in this way that we seek here to link the kinds of future-oriented utopian aspirations of the past to educational discourses and practices in the present. For Foucault (1977), a central task in writing history is to think anew about both the past and the present, to investigate the present not as the inevitable outcome of the past. Genealogy is interested in questions about specificity and in how the present and past are different rather than in how the present unfolds from the past. As such, it favours a narrative of discontinuity rather than one of continuity and repetition. By drawing out what is specific about both the past and the present, this approach also has practical benefits, showing how 'problems' are defined or arise and the kind of responses they generate (O'Farrell 2005).

Two decades ago, a special issue of the journal *History of Education Review* edited by Johnson and Tyler (1991) called for a reinvigoration of the history of education, making a strong case for Foucauldian-inspired conceptual approaches to investigating a 'history of the present'. In their opening essay, 'Helpful histories?', Tyler and Johnson (1991) argued that the significance of these approaches is in 'making the present strange rather than the past familiar' (p. 5). Much history of education, they argued, was concerned about any perceived 'presentism' in historical writing, regarding attention to 'contemporary pre-occupations' as detracting from the proper business of history – recreating 'the past in its proper setting' – and risking anachronistic accounts that judge the past by the standards of the present (p. 3). For Tyler and Johnson, the challenge lay precisely in re-imagining the past–present relation, including taking account 'of the role of history writing in producing what counts as knowledge in the present' (p. 3).

Tyler and Johnson's important essay, and the special issue as a whole, captured an interesting moment in the history of theoretical and historical writing in Australian educational research. Despite there now being a body of clearly identifiable Foucauldian research in education, many of the challenges raised in this earlier issue remain pertinent, with some inadequately realised, even in research which purports to be Foucauldian (Butchart 2011, Coloma 2011). Over the last two decades, the marked enthusiasm for Foucauldian concepts and approaches in educational research has been most evident in more sociologically oriented rather than historical research (Baker 2007, McLeod 2009). Governmentality, for example, has become largely a study of the present. Within the field of history of education, there has been some renewed debate on the value and risks of Foucauldian scholarship and some critical reflection on what its effects have been and what it has offered, and can offer, historical studies on education (e.g. Tamura *et al.* 2011). We are arguing here for the value of pushing Foucauldian scholarship in education towards a more sustained problematisation of the past–present relationship, rather than simply using the past as a means of critically analysing the present. Some of the larger issues raised by Tyler and Johnson frame our discussion here, as we modestly start to understand the relation between past and present-day constructions of students, teachers and citizens of the future, as well as the history of discourses of hope and optimism in educational thinking and practices.

In reflecting on temporality and feminist theory, Grosz (2010) has observed that the predominant orientation of feminist scholarship has been to look to the past or to the present, to take these as the primary focus of enquiry. Consequently, she suggests, feminism has not been sufficiently attuned to the future, to grappling with 'the force of temporality' (p. 51). Grosz argues that: 'One of the central questions of contemporary feminist theory as it faces a changing future, as it directs itself to the question of change, should be about what is *untimely*, what is out of its time' (p. 48). Conversely, we might argue that educational research and discourse have been characterised by a pre-occupation with future possibilities, of dreams of better things to come, of imagining education as it otherwise could be. This has been accompanied in recent years with evidence of declining interest in historical studies of education (Campbell and Sherington 2002, McCulloch 2011). Looking to the 'untimely' in education perhaps involves a more robust engagement, not so much with the future, but with the past and with the past–present relation, leading us to ask how looking back at utopian sentiments shapes how we might understand and act in the educational present: this is a background question for this special issue.

The articles in this special issue began as a symposium held at the 2010 conference of the Australian Association for Research in Education. The symposium explored 'the promise of the new' in educational history, with a view to thinking afresh about the ways in which problems of youth, nation and schooling are constructed and educational reform espoused, both historically and in the present. On the whole, the articles examine published texts and authoritative discourses circulating at the time, rather than new archival sources. The aim has been to explore expert or formal advice, aspiration and commentary, to look at the ways in which calls for the new were embedded in mainstream discussions, not on the fringe, or in marginal or so-called radical discourses. While the articles each address different topics – adolescence, teachers, guidance, internationalism and curriculum – threaded through them are concerns about the construction of citizens and non-citizens, race and difference, and the classification and education of emerging populations of insiders and outsiders within the new nation.

In the opening article, Phil Cormack examines some of the key challenges that arose with the expansion of post-primary schooling in Australia. By the 1920s, he argues, the adolescent population had become a new focus of governmental concern, with compulsory schooling being the articulation of a range of social projects and hopes and ideals for the youth of the day. Cormack draws on the Foucauldian concept of *dispositif* to explicate the argument that this was not an organised and rational social project, but rather reflected a coalescence of disparate social initiatives, emerging practices of government and more diffuse socio-cultural ideals and aspirations for young people. Within this context of the expansion of compulsory post-primary schooling, however, there arose a problem: what to do with those 'pupils differently circumstanced and with other aims'. To examine this issue, Cormack analyses a key text of the 1920s, *Education in Australia: a comparative study of the educational systems of the six Australian states* (Browne 1927). The central question his article addresses is, 'In what way were these young people of 12–15 years a problem of and for education?' As Cormack demonstrates, the identification of educational problems in the text was also couched in terms of an optimistic discourse of educational progress and the need for Australia – with its 'vast hinterland' – to develop educational solutions different from those of Europe and America. Cormack acknowledges that there are strong echoes of the present in the subject of his article – disengagement, curriculum alternatives and adolescence as a problem for schools. However, rather than his primary aim being to problematise the present, Cormack considers what 'shadows' his inquiry might throw on the past. Through the lens of the subject English, he argues that the curricula which developed around the different versions of schooling established for this problem population became articulated with competing discourses of educational psychology, talent and culture, each of which continues to shape secondary school curriculum to this day.

In the following article, Katie Wright explores the way in which new psychologically based knowledges and techniques were used to target a more specific range of emerging educational and social problems. Framed within the context of a broader approach to the individualising of education, she documents the development of various forms of 'guidance' in Australian state schooling systems. Vocational guidance was introduced to help young people to identify their calling and secure employment, educational guidance was developed to assist with post-primary selection and placement, and child guidance clinics were established for the treatment of emotional, psychological and behavioural problems. In its various forms, guidance held the promise of ameliorating intractable social and economic problems: vocational and educational guidance provided the means to avoid inefficiency, while child guidance held the promise of preventing 'maladjustment' and delinquency. Wright demonstrates how international ideas and practices, particularly those associated with progressive education and the so-called new psychology, shaped Australian developments. While vocational guidance has most readily been associated with the guidance movement, Wright argues that it is also important to consider other forms of guidance that emerged in Australia at this time. This involves examining the common aims of different forms of guidance, in particular, the promise of prevention that inspired the movement, as well as the various ways in which this broad vision took institutional form:

the school as site of state-sponsored guidance, the privately controlled guidance bureau, and the child guidance clinic as a provider of multidisciplinary mental health services for young people. An examination of the guidance movement in this broader sense points to the critical place of psychological knowledge in the expanding role of schools and other agencies in managing the development of children and adolescents and guiding them towards adulthood.

The internationalist outlook that pervaded educational discussions and the influence of psychological approaches, particularly mental testing, are also highlighted in Julie McLeod's article. The focus of her analysis is ideas about citizenship education and learning to be a citizen in the interwar years in Australia and the differentiated and racialised possibilities afforded for becoming and being regarded as a proper citizen. Drawing on genealogical approaches and accounts of cosmopolitanism, she explores these issues through the juxtaposition of two international conferences of the 1930s: *Education in Pacific Countries*, held in Hawaii in 1936; and *The Fellowship of Education: education for complete living*, which took place in Australia in 1937. Both conferences were concerned with the philosophical and instructional purposes of education, the organisation and function of formal schooling, and the education and educability of young Australians. As she shows, discussion at both conferences elaborated the attributes of a good student and a good citizen and on what constituted responsible education towards and for citizenship. Both conferences espoused the benefits of an internationalist outlook and comparative understanding in opening up new ideas for the education of young people. Yet, as she reveals, there were significant differences in how issues of internationalism, adolescent capacity and the hopeful possibilities for future education and citizenship were articulated, particularly in relation to Australians of so-called British stock and the educability of Indigenous Australians. What emerges in McLeod's analysis is how this 'new citizen' was ideally to be cosmopolitan in orientation, able to cultivate 'the habit of independent thought and opinion' and respect different points of view. What is also revealed, however, are the dividing practices of the new cosmopolitanism and the gendered and racialised silences in this conception of a self-consciously new kind of [adolescent] subject. Adolescence was a blossoming for white children, an opening up of the possibilities of rationality and independence of mind. As far as Aboriginal children were imagined, however, it signalled the decline of possibilities and a time when bodily and hormonal drives and kin relations and responsibilities took over.

In Bill Green and Jo-Anne Reid's article, the newly federated nation of Australia and its hopes and aspirations for its future citizens take centre stage. Their article focuses on the expansion of public schooling and the importance of developing a new kind of teacher for the new nation. As they note in the beginning of their article, during the early years of the twentieth century, there was much consternation about the quality of teachers in Australia, with suggestions even that they were the 'least educated in the English-speaking world'. This presented a major problem for national progress, an issue that is brought into sharp relief in recent historiography, which suggests that teacher identity and national identity are thoroughly intertwined. Green and Reid argue that emerging populations of children and young people in need of secondary education formed a new constituency that in turn demanded a new and improved kind of teacher and concomitantly a new system of teacher education, framed in accordance with what was widely understood as the New Education. Developments in teacher education throughout the first half of the twentieth century, they argue, were clearly conceived to be in the service of nation-building and the primary focus on improving the quality of Australian teachers was the subject of English. Indeed, they suggest that the cultural and ideological significance of the teaching of English was central to broader aspirations about nation and empire. This was reflected further in the importance attached to the English language throughout all facets of schooling and in the emphasis on promulgating 'Englishness' and the capacity to speak the 'mother tongue' well. Australian slang was to be eradicated, and to achieve this, they note, *every* teacher needed indeed to become and be 'a teacher of English', at every level of schooling and across all subject areas. As Green and Reid argue, a central dimension of the professionalisation of teaching and teacher education during the early twentieth century centred upon English. And it was therefore increasingly incumbent upon teachers to work on their accents and habits of speech if they were to attain the authority and respect of both the pupils within their charge and the authorities prescribing these new appropriate standards for educators.

In the final article, Maxine Stephenson reflects on the themes raised in the special issue, teasing out their implications for the history of educational reform and administration. She looks beyond Australia to consider these matters in comparative and international contexts, focusing on related developments in New Zealand's educational history. Stephenson's discussion on the politics of biology underscores the influence of eugenics throughout the Antipodes and, in doing so, extends the frame of reference for discussions about the importance of scientific knowledges that run throughout each of the articles in this issue. She reminds us that prominent eugenicists, along with their powerful political allies in the fields of medicine, psychiatry, psychology, statistics, criminology and social work, were instrumental in the promulgation of new discourses of national efficiency and racial fitness. Such discourses had, as Stephenson argues, important ramifications for the organisation of schooling. The transnational outlook characteristic of such discourses and the development of professional networks beyond national borders are also explored through her analysis of the New Education Fellowship. As she notes, with meetings held in the Antipodes during the 1930s, it appeared that 'Australia and New Zealand were joining the big players'. Progressive education was high on the agenda, shaping a variety of reforms and new initiatives, from new approaches to the classification of students to the professionalisation of teachers and the need for new kinds of schools. In New Zealand, an important development in this area was new policy directions pertaining to 'Native Schools' and the importance of 'culture' and its preservation. As Stephenson suggests, many factors were at play in this shifting policy landscape, but an important dimension was the politicisation of a group of young Māori concerned about the role of schooling in the marginalisation of cultural and political rights. This discussion provides an interesting counterpoint to the kinds of discussions taking place in Australia at this time, particularly in relation to the perceived educability of Aboriginal children. In these examples, as with the rest of her essay and in the other contributions to this special issue, important directions and possibilities are opened up for further exploration of the intersection of hope, optimism and histories of the present.

Acknowledgements

We extend our thanks to the authors of this issue for their contributions, the anonymous referees for their valuable comments and insightful suggestions, and the editors of this journal, Helen Gunter and Tanya Fitzgerald, for their support in making this special issue possible. For editorial assistance, we also offer our thanks to Amy McKernan.

References

Baker, B., 2007. Normalizing Foucault? A rhizomatic approach to plateaus in anglophone educational research. *Foucault studies*, 4 (February), 78–119.

Brehony, K., 2000. Montessori, individual work and individuality in the elementary classroom. *History of education*, 29 (2), 115–128.

Browne, G.S., ed., 1927. *Education in Australia: a comparative study of the educational systems of six Australian states*. London: Macmillan.

Butchart, R.E., 2011. What's Foucualt got to do with it? History, theory and becoming subjected. *History of education quarterly*, 51 (2), 239–246.

Campbell, C. and Sherington, G., 2002. The history of education: the possibility of survival. *Change: transformations in education*, 5 (1), 46–64.

Cole, P.R., ed., 1935. *The education of the adolescent in Australia*. Vol. 32. Melbourne: Melbourne University Press.

Coloma, R.S., 2011. Who's afraid of Foucault? History, theory and becoming subjects. *History of education quarterly*, 51 (2), 184–210.

Foucault, M., 1977. Nietzsche, genealogy, history. *In*: D.F. Bouchard, ed. *Language, counter-memory, practice: selected essays and interviews*. Ithaca, NY: Cornell University Press, 139–164.

Grosz, E., 2010. The untimeliness of feminist theory. *NORA – Nordic journal of feminist and gender research*, 18 (1), 48–51.

Halpin, D., 2003. *Hope and education: the role of the utopian imagination.* London: Routledge.

Johnson, L. and Tyler, D., eds., 1991. Special issue. *History of education review*, 20 (2).

McCulloch, G., 2011. *The struggle for the history of education.* London: Routledge.

McLeod, J., 2009. What *was* poststructural feminism in education? *In*: M.W. Apple, W. Au, and L.A. Gandin, eds. *Routledge international handbook of critical education.* New York: Routledge, 137–149.

O'Farrell, C., 2005. *Michel Foucault.* London: Sage.

Tamura, E., Eick, C., and Coloma, R., 2011. Theory in educational history. Special issue. *History of education quarterly*, 51 (2), 148–149.

Tyler, D. and Johnson, L., 1991. Helpful histories? *History of education review*, 20 (2), 1–8.

Webb, D., 2009. Where's the vision? The concept of utopia in contemporary educational theory. *Oxford review of education*, 35 (6), 743–760.

'Pupils differently circumstanced and with other aims': governing the post-primary child in early twentieth-century Australia

Phil Cormack

School of Education, University of South Australia, Magill, Australia

> Writing in 1927, five leading scholars and administrators of the Australian schooling systems published a book entitled *Education in Australia: a comparative study of the educational systems of the six Australian states*. These authors wrote of Australian education in a time of great optimism, and one of the key areas of reform they addressed was the introduction of forms of post-primary schooling for a 'problem' population of 12–15-year-olds who were not attracted to, or staying with, the high school curriculum which led towards university study. Through the lens of *Education in Australia*, this paper undertakes a genealogical exploration of the way the adolescent emerged as an object of school reforms in the early twentieth century and shows that these reforms were articulated with discourses of race, social efficiency, science and culture.

Introduction

In 1927, five leading scholars and administrators of the Australian state schooling systems published a book entitled *Education in Australia: a comparative study of the educational systems of the six Australian states* (Browne 1927d). Constitutionally, each Australian state was responsible for the curriculum and provision of schooling within its borders and fulfilled that responsibility through state-wide departments of education, which are described in the book's introduction as 'the most strongly centralised systems of educational administration in the world' (Browne 1927b, p. xvii). These authors were writing at a time of the expansion of Australian school education beyond the primary schools that had been established in the last quarter of the nineteenth century and in a time of optimism and reform for Australian schooling. This book was, according to the editor's introduction, the first detailed examination of schooling across the nation (p. xvii) and, as such, attended to the issues and 'problems' which it was felt faced education across the newly established nation. Far from being critical of the centralised nature of educational administration, Browne argued that it was 'the best form of educational rule for a young country with a vast hinterland' (p. xvii), indicating that the 'unique' geography and history of the nation required educational solutions that were different from those which worked in Europe and America. Six of the eight chapters, using a near-common structure, tell each state's 'story of marked educational progress and flexibility of administration' (p. xvii) while outlining its approaches to addressing contemporary challenges and problems.

One of the key 'problems' at that time, according to this book, was that the limited state post-primary schooling then available was missing the mark with a significant proportion of young people who were not attracted to, or staying with, the high school curriculum that led towards university study. As the Principal of the Teachers' College in Adelaide wrote in his chapter on South Australia (Schulz 1927, p. 200), these were 'pupils differently circumstanced and with other aims'. So significant was this issue that most state chapters included a section entitled 'The twelve to fifteen problem',[1] signalling that this focus was one built into the design of the book as a concern across the nation. The question I wish to address here is: In what way were these young people of a particular age a problem of and for education? Moreover, what can be learnt from these accounts from between the major world wars of the twentieth century that might help us think about the education of adolescents today?

Education in Australia is unremarkable in one sense in that it can be seen as a typical modernist account of progress and reform, explaining educational practices as rational responses to the policy goals and contexts of its time. Read in this way, such a text is a historical curio, relevant to educational historians perhaps, but with little to say to current educators in a different time and context. However, considered genealogically in relation to the present, this text is a reminder of some compelling and uncomfortable continuities which help to estrange some of the taken-for-granted ways of thinking about the schooling of adolescents. Rather than attempting to throw some 'light' on the present, this paper considers what 'shadows' are thrown by the past on our present ways of thinking or what remains hidden, unremarked or only seen in the periphery of our policy gaze. In Baker's (2004) terms, it contributes to a 'glancing' history of public education:

> A glancing history captures and fails to capture completely the complex intertwining of identities produced, circulated, forgotten and remembered in public schooling's formation. It does this in the form of looking askance from dominant interpretations of education's past and with regard to the kinds of deflections thought necessary to define something or someone as public. (p. 9)

In many ways, *Education in Australia* can be seen as a key moment in Australian educational history in defining the whole population of 12–15-year-olds (or 'adolescents') as being a 'public', or governmental, concern and therefore 'needing' compulsory schooling. This paper analyses the way the problem of the older child, or 'adolescent', was articulated in *Education in Australia* and traces some of the key discourses that constituted this thinking. I argue that this articulation was not a conscious social programme but more a crystallisation, at a moment in time, of various parallel, even contradictory, social projects, practices of government, ideals and hopes into what, nevertheless, became an apparently seamless programme for preparing adolescents for their future lives. This process has been described by Foucault (1991) as 'disorderly' and as a kind of bundling of disparate programmes into an apparently 'solid' and flexible set of arrangements which he labelled a *dispositif*.[2] In the next section, I begin this analysis by showing the importance of the concept of 'race' in providing a warrant for social programmes connected to the adolescent.

Schooling in a white, isolated, British nation: adolescence as the future of the race

Browne's introduction to the book lays out the key parameters for thinking about the education of the nation. It is a text marked by a strong sense of satisfaction in the 'progress' that had been made up to the 1920s, especially in forming a secular public school system at the primary level. Schools were linked, via an educational 'ladder', to universities through high schools for a small percentage of the population, with scholarships to provide access to the 'able' poor. Looking to the future with some optimism; for 'Australia is as yet only at the beginning of her educational road' (1927b, p. xxi), Browne promised a 'very responsible task' for Australian teachers: 'that of guiding this great British nation in the south through the critical years of its youth' (p. xxi). In this way, Browne hailed an important trope in the construction of the nation's history, casting Australia as youthful and energetic while positioning it as an Antipodean outpost of empire and the (white) hope for its future.

A key discourse in the book's introduction is that of race, whereby the future of the nation and the role of educators in ensuring its progress are linked to its Britishness as a genetic, cultural and administrative enterprise:

> It should be remembered that *Australia's educational problem* is unlike that of any other nation. Here is a whole continent as large as the United States and nearly as large as Europe. As yet it contains only six million people, but these people are almost entirely of British stock. There is no native problem owing to the fact that the aboriginal inhabitants have nearly disappeared. There is practically no foreign element in the population. Yet the northern shores of Australia are only a few days' sail from overwhelming millions of coloured peoples. Can she keep her continent white? Can she carry through a progressive immigration policy? With so small a population dispersed over such an immense area, can her States develop and maintain effective systems of education? (Browne 1927b, p. xviii, emphasis added)

Here, issues of population, space and race are bundled, connected to the very survival of the (British) nation, and labelled as 'Australia's educational problem'. The question is, how could such a connection be made in a text where the education of a population of 12–14/15-year-olds was so prominent?

To explore, historically, this connection within education between nation, race and adolescence is to acknowledge a number of significant relationships between theories of development and race and between science and education. While the explicit racialism obvious in Browne's editorial is unacceptable today, related logics remain significant and somewhat uncomfortable continuities to the present. In what follows, I explore the ways that racial thinking and adolescence were linked in the early twentieth century and made it possible to think of the education of 12–15-year-olds as a key problem for the nation. I then go on to consider the programmes of reform that were taken up by the authors of *Education in Australia* to explore the way that a range of discourses intersected with those of race to inform educational thinking at that time and beyond.

Race and adolescence

The early twentieth century was a time of considerable anxiety about the future of the Empire and of the 'fitness' of the modern British subject in what was commonly referred to at that time as 'the world's race' (Mosely Educational Commission 1904, p. xiv). Responding to the emergence of the USA as a commercial power and the rising influence of Germany, as well as its own defeat in the Boer War, there was a great deal of concern in Britain and its colonies about the future of the Empire. These concerns were also related to Darwinian conceptions of survival and fitness of races and the understanding that some species flourished and then died out due to competition. Combined with recapitulationist theories of growth, which cast the growth of the individual from birth to maturity as recapitulating the growth and development of a species, these provided a space for anxiety about the child and adolescent as properly growing, becoming proper, 'fit' individuals who would thereby ensure the future of the race and nation.

In her study of adolescence, Lesko (2001) explores the way that adolescence was connected to narratives of growth in the nineteenth century. For her, the idea of progress, built on science and its other – disease and decay, came to be embodied in adolescence as a:

> space for reformers to talk about their worries and fears and a space for public policy to enact new ideas for creating citizens and a nation that could lead and dominate the particular problems and opportunities of the modern world. (Lesko 2001, p. 21)

One of the defining metaphors available at the end of the nineteenth century, according to Lesko (2001), was the progress of life as represented by the 'Great Chain of Being':

> The Great Chain of Being refers to the hierarchy of animals, people, and societies that portrayed evolutionary history and a sociological ranking extending from European middle-class males and their republican government on the top, through women to savage tribes, with the lower animals at the bottom. There was also a moral, or spiritual, dimension to this Great Chain of Being, that is, the movement from lower to higher levels also signified the movement from chaos through human law to divine law. (p. 22)

This concept of progress came to form an integrating function, able to pull together into a simple narrative ideas from anthropology, psychology, biology and medicine. As well as representing ideas of progress, this narrative also contained fears about the possibility of decline – it allowed for movements in both directions along the chain.

Fears about the fitness of the race and its ability to sustain the future of the nation can be seen in a range of programmes and reforms that were undertaken in England, America and Australia. This work allowed for the population to become calculable in terms of military and economic strength and for the promotion of health and education that facilitated the development of norms for individuals, families and communities. Concepts of race, at this time, could also act metonymically as a statement about the people of the nation or empire. If the race/nation/empire was to achieve progress – to become even more advanced and civilised – then the period of adolescence was the place for the race to pull itself up by its own evolutionary bootstraps. As 'the father of adolescence', G. Stanley Hall (1904) said in his two-volume book on adolescence:

> [F]or those prophetic souls interested in the future of our race and desirous of advancing it, the field of adolescence is the quarry in which they must seek to find both goal and means. If such a higher stage is ever added to our race, it will not be by increments at any later plateau of adult life, but it will come by increased development of the adolescent stage, which is the bud and the promise for the race. (p. 531)

This idea of adolescence being 'the promise for the race' would heighten this developmental stage as a site of anxiety in terms of the future of the nation, especially in relation to reproduction and population. Some 'men' were seen to inherit a degenerate 'germ' which prevented proper social and intellectual abilities and which could be passed on to subsequent generations. As Baker (2001, p. 538) says, degeneration was closely related to the idea of 'miscegenation', which was the fear of mixing with other, more 'savage', races ('how can we keep Australia white?') and thereby inheriting their defects. Adolescence, as the age at which sexual reproduction became possible, but also as something that was ontologically connected with the savage, became the category in which this anxiety could be grounded as needing to be monitored and controlled.

Interestingly, in the name of vigorously expanding and building new nations and empires, the savagery inherent in the young could be seen as a resource as well as a problem, for it indicated a spirit of risk and energy that could be the building blocks of future evolutionary development. Adolescence, then, was a time of necessary 'storm and stress': a time when racial progress or degeneration came together as possibilities, and a period that needed appropriate monitoring and guidance towards adulthood via schooling specifically designed for this stage. This was a strong trope in the Australian education scene of the 1920s, which can be tracked through a range of intertextual links from *Education in Australia*.

Beginning with the chapter on Victoria written by the book editor, Browne (1927c, p. 110) quotes directly from a study comparing the Victorian and Scottish school systems with a focus on the education of the 12–15-year-old. The study cited by Samson (1925) was entitled: *A comparison of Scottish and Victorian education, shewing in particular that Victoria can derive much benefit from a study of the type of education given in Scottish schools between the ages of twelve and fifteen*. In that study, Samson himself makes the argument for such schooling, in part, based on racialised arguments. Samson cites the statement that '[t]he community that starves itself of education sterilises itself' (p. 150), which is a quotation from the *Report of the Chief Inspector of secondary schools: on educational systems and administration and especially on secondary and continued education in England and America* (Hansen 1923). The Victorian Chief Inspector in question was Peter Hansen, who wrote the report after a trip overseas in 1922–1923. Hansen became the Victorian Assistant Director of Education in 1927 and Director in 1928 (Blake 1973). By the time Browne became the Principal of the Teachers' College in Melbourne, Hansen would be his manager.

The intertextual references ripple back to a similar report written in 1908 by the South Australian Director of Education Alfred Williams (at that time, manager of Adolf Schulz, who wrote the chapter on South Australia in *Education in Australia*). Just before the quotation on sterilisation, Hansen's report included a reference to adolescence as a time 'when character is formed, habits acquired and the whole line of life settled' – an echo of a quotation in Williams' report, as follows:

> Education is not for labour only, but for life; and the years between 13 and 17 are the critical and formative years for every human being. Then the physical energies of the body, as in a spring tide, thrill out in every limb and organ. Then the callow brood of instinctive desires, both intellectual and social, are agape, and young native faculties shoot out in rapid, random growth. Then, if ever, is the need for education to guide, restrain, and inspire. In these years *character is formed and destiny made almost unalterably*. (Dr Paton, quoted in Williams 1908, emphasis added)

The so-called *Hadow Report* on the education of adolescents in England was published in the same year as *Education in Australia* and itself picked up on this theme of destiny in the blood, tapping into the strength and energy of adolescence as a way of ensuring 'fortune' for the nation:

> There is a tide which begins to rise in the *veins* of youth at the age of eleven or twelve. It is called by the name of adolescence. If that tide can be taken at the flood, and a new voyage begun in the strength and along the flow of the current, we think that it will 'move on to fortune'. (Consultative Committee of the Board of Education [The *Hadow Report*] 1927, p. xix, emphasis added)

Seven years later, Australia was to have its own version of the Hadow Report, written by a 'Committee on the Education of the Adolescent in Australia' (Cole 1935) under the auspices of the Australian Council for Educational Research and made up of senior educational administrators including, as editor and chair, the same Percival Cole who wrote in *Education in Australia*. Also among the authors was H.T. Lovell, the first Professor of the first Department of Psychology in Australia, at Sydney University. His explanation of evolution referred to 'race preservation' and 'self preservation' as the drivers of adolescent behaviour where the 'higher spiritual welfare of cultural beings may require their subordination, and will certainly require their modification' (Lovell 1935, p. 63). This linkage between the (irresistible) drive for racial preservation in the adolescent and the need for *culture* to manage its dangers will be returned to below.

This brief intertextual excursion shows that racialised and biological understandings of adolescence, expressed through references to blood, veins and the irresistible forces of the flood and tide, were influential forms of thinking about young people of this age, as needing education to 'guide, restrain, and inspire', to use William's words, to build the nation's future. At the same time, as Bessant (1991) argues, eugenics was a respectable and prominent theory of racial improvement within the field of education:

> This discourse was the work of a network of international and domestic 'child savers', educationists, researchers, social workers, psychologists who since the turn of the century had developed an extensive literature about 'maladjusted young people'. At the heart of this discourse was eugenics and its themes of scientific measurement, social functionalism and biological determinism, psychological adjustment and racial fitness. These eugenic themes were promoted and affirmed overtly until the end of the Second World War, and somewhat more covertly after 1945. (pp. 12–13)

This notion of adolescence as a crucial stage of progress upon which the future competitiveness of a nation (if not the race) depends is a narrative with strong continuities into the present – for example, that adolescence is the 'last best chance' to ensure a better future is a concept used in the first paragraph of the influential Carnegie Council on Adolescent Development middle schooling report, *Turning Points* (Carnegie Council on Adolescent Development 1989, p. 8), and these ideas continue to resonate in more contemporary discourses on middle schooling.

Of course, race was not the only discourse evident in the design of the book, but it clearly was an important site for anxiety. Its inclusion in the introduction to *Education in Australia* shows how central this issue was to aspirations and fears for the nation's future. It is also in this context that the 12–15-year-old was singled out as a problem of the first order for the nation. The next section examines the ways that the authors addressed the problem of the 12–15-year-old in the context of the education systems they described.

How the 12–15 problem was situated

Considered here are the four chapters in which the 12–15 problem was explicitly treated – on New South Wales (NSW) by Percival R. Cole, who was Vice-Principal and lecturer in education at the Teachers' College, Sydney, from 1910 to 1940; on Victoria by G.S. Browne himself, Vice-Principal of Melbourne Teachers' College, appointed principal of the College and Professor of Education at University of Melbourne in 1933; on South Australia by Adolf J. Schulz, who was, from 1909 to 1948, Principal of Adelaide Teachers' College; and on Western Australia by Wallace Clubb, who was a senior Inspector and Director of Education in that state from 1930. Each of these four chapters, along with those from the other two states which did not feature the 12–15 problem heading, followed the pattern (with small variations) shown in Table 1, which gives the headings used by Schulz in the South Australian chapter.

The overall structure shown in Table 1 is a reflection of the scope of the powerful administrative structure that had been established in Australia in just 50 years

Table 1. Headings in the South Australian chapter.

(1)	Brief historical sketch
(2)	Organisation and administration of the national system
(3)	Conspectus showing scheme of public education in South Australia
(4)	Private and denominational schools
(5)	Development of infant schools
(6)	Primary schools
(7)	The 'twelve to fifteen' problem
(8)	Secondary schools
(9)	Vocational schools and continued education
(10)	Special schools
(11)	Medical and dental services
(12)	Experimental work
(13)	Supply, classification and training of teachers
(14)	Inspection, examinations and scholarships
(15)	The university
(16)	Forecast of educational developments during the next ten years

since the passing of the education acts in the colonies. Each state had compulsory education for students up to 14 years old (extended from 12 years old during the Great War in most states), and the authors were clearly optimistic that it would soon be raised to age 15, although, in fact, the Depression intervened and this did not occur in most states until 1942. At the other end of the scale, there was a university and a technical institution for professional education, as well as a teachers' college. Between the primary school and tertiary institutions, there was a high school system for the small number of students who would 'climb the educational ladder', although the private system rather than the state carried much of that population. However, these were systems that were largely in place by the end of the first decade of the century (Cormack 2004); what was new here, and connected to the 12–15 problem, was the inclusion of vocational schools and special schools – in other words, the expansion of schooling to those who were considered beyond the scope of education systems when they were first established.

Cole, in his chapter on NSW, illustrates the way in which 'science' had made it thinkable for the state to educate those who were previously judged not suitable for schooling, noting in relation to the 'physically afflicted' that:

> [b]efore 1900 little scientific attempt was made to treat them as educable though there were institutions – homes of a charitable more than of an educative nature for the deaf, dumb and blind, supported mainly by the precarious resources of charity. (1927, p. 52)

Now in relation to the 'mentally defective', for example, a 'promising movement' had been established in Sydney, with 'eight special classes, set apart for mental defectives, supervised by an expert psychologist'. This, he noted, gave 'promise of a coming era of achievement' for such students (p. 53).

Such claims are illustrative of the way that the optimism of progressive educational thinkers in the early twentieth century was underpinned by a faith in scientific knowledge. The emerging technology of educational testing arrayed whole populations within a bell-shaped curve and made it possible to imagine the management of formerly problematic groups within schools.[3] In this way, the whole population, suitably diagnosed and scientifically managed, could be imagined as amenable to the education process. The inclusion of the 12–15 problem section in these educational outlines needs to be seen as part of a larger process which included the introduction of medical and psychological branches, the consolidation of special education and the proliferation of alternative forms of education for non-tertiary bound older children. Consider the following subheadings from the section on 'Special Schools' in Browne's (1927c) chapter on Victoria: (a) Feeble-Minded Children; (b) The Correspondence Branch; (c) Deaf and Dumb Children; (d) Blind Children; (e) Epileptic Children; (f) Recuperative School; (g) Itinerant Teachers; and (h) Subsidised Schools.

This list shows that the whole child population was being brought within the care and control of education and not just those who were formerly institutionalised. As is shown by the inclusion of the 'Correspondence Branch' and 'Itinerant' teachers, even those children in the isolated parts of rural Australia were to be included in state provisions of education. Defined in terms of their needs by science, and assigned their various specialist sites of expertise, the education of each aspect of the adolescent population had become a problem of administration. Each of the four authors described the way in which the specialist treatment of the 12–15-year-olds was a key to a proper education. This was because of their difference from the primary school child, as in this description by Clubb (1927):

> An education that ends with the Primary School ends just when the golden years of adolescence begin – the golden years in which the teacher's greatest opportunity comes, the years when the boy or girl begins to appreciate for the first time the bigger problems of life .... (p. 345)

More importantly, it was also due to the differences among adolescents themselves, or especially to those 'pupils differently circumstanced and with other aims', as Schulz put it, when differentiating these problem students from those who 'intended to proceed to the University or to enter the ranks of the professionals ...' (p. 200). For Browne in Victoria, these were 12–15-year-olds whose 'future occupations will lie in commerce, arts and crafts, trade, factory work and unskilled labour' (p. 107). Cole (1927), in NSW, added girls to this group by claiming that these adolescents included those who would 'join the ranks of workers in industry, in commerce, *or in domestic arts*' (emphasis added, p. 39).

There were three sub-populations of adolescents described by these educationalists. The first was that (small) group which attended the high school and was intending on sitting university set exams – the future leaders of the society. The second group consisted of those who left as soon as they turned 14 or soon after, 'just when the golden years of adolescence begin', as Clubb put it. The third group consisted of those who moved on to the post-primary schools established by the state but who found the curriculum on offer to be less than useful or attractive. Schulz in South Australia noted that 'of many pupils who did enter, not a few left after receiving but a single year of additional schooling' (1927, p. 200). It was these last two groups that were the focus of the authors' concern and who constituted the 12–15 problem, and social class was the key differentiator. The children of the working classes who needed their children to earn an income, or who saw an academic education as unsuited to their futures on the farm, or in other semi-skilled or unskilled work, were the target of these reformers.

The racialised discourse of adolescence gave additional purchase to the idea that a dedicated educational space was needed for the 12–15-year-olds, but within this space these reformers argued for differentiated provision according to the futures that these children were destined to take up. This gave rise to a tension – one that remains in secondary schooling to this day – between the treatment of this age group as a whole, which must be harnessed for the sake of national (and racial/imperial) progress, and the need to govern the sub-populations within this group according to different aspirations and fears. The next section considers some of the projects of reform that were promoted by the authors of *Education in Australia* to manage this age group and its sub-populations.

Projects of reform: intersections of the new and the old

Both new and well-established discourses of education were present in constituting how these educators imagined that adolescents could be shaped as ideal citizens. Some of the well-established discourses were those of 'social efficiency' and 'culture', while some of the newer ways of thinking involved the application of scientific thinking via educational psychology that incorporated views of adolescence as a 'stage' of development – and each could be connected with a dominant discourse of race. These were overlapping and even inconsistent logics and practices, rather than a singular vision operating to shape the ideals for reform, much as a *dispositif* is described by Foucault (1991, p. 181) as 'different strategies which are mutually opposed, composed and superposed so as to produce permanent and solid effects which can perfectly well be understood in terms of their rationality, even though they don't conform to the initial programming'.

Whatever their ideals and practices, each of these programmes of reform faced a number of daunting challenges when it came to the expansion of schooling to a whole new population and age group. These challenges included, to name some of the most obvious: the management of a population over vast distances; selection and distribution of the population into different pathways and sites; and how to incorporate new sections of the population into schools not designed with their aspirations in mind. As I sketch each of these reform programmes below, it can be seen that the programmes had different ideals and strategies for addressing such challenges and that none was sufficient on its own. It is important to see them as overlapping, even contradictory, yet able, as an ensemble, to produce reforms which established the basis of compulsory state secondary schooling for all adolescents. Three key social programmes (Green 2005) and their associated discourses are Social Efficiency, Culture and Educational Psychology.

So that 'society can maximally profit': Social Efficiency

An important logic behind the plans discussed above was 'Social Efficiency', a social and economic programme that aimed, through a science of administration, to provide the appropriate education to pupils depending on their 'ability' and/or destination in life. Social Efficiency was a movement born out of turn-of-the-twentieth-century sociological theories of social control and Taylorist scientific theories of factory management (Kliebard 1995). Broadly speaking, it was a 'science of exact measurement and precise standards in the interests of maintaining a predictable and orderly world' (p. 77). Social Efficiency connected the government of young people to the great 'competition' between the peoples and nations of the world. The term 'efficient' had a meaning somewhat similar to the present-day terms 'productivity' and 'effectiveness' in relation to education. Schulz (1927, p. 235), for example, could talk about the way that annual examinations by Inspectors could measure the 'efficiency' of schools. Efficiency was also connected to the avoidance of 'wastage'. Within the discourse of Social Efficiency, every child had a *capacity* that could be trained and the job of post-primary education was to *fit* the child to the work for which he or she had such a capacity. The 1908 report cited above by the South Australian Director Alfred Williams outlined this form of thinking clearly, quoting the eminent American educator William Bagley:

> Social efficiency is the standard by which the forces of education must select the experiences that are to be impressed upon the individual. Every subject of instruction, every item of knowledge, every form of reaction, every detail of habit, must be measured by this yardstick. Not what pleasure will this bring the individual, not in what manner will this contribute to his harmonious development, not what effect will this have upon his bread-winning capacity; but always, will this subject, or this knowledge, or this reaction, or this habit so function in his after-life that society will maximally profit? ('Dr Bagley', quoted in Williams 1908, p. 13)

The key strategy for managing the fitting of the child to 'his after-life' involved the establishment of different versions of post-primary schooling for 12–15-year-olds who were not aiming at university study. This meant that the already established state high schools serving the children of the emerging middle class, and the private colleges serving the children of the well-off, remained untouched and garnered the distinction of leading their students to the most prestigious occupations (Campbell 1995, Campbell *et al.* 1999) – a distinction against which the newly established schools for the 'differently circumstanced' were always to be judged. These new schools included 'Central Schools', which Schulz (1927, p. 178) explained were established in 1925 as 'extensions of existing large primary schools, with separate departments for boys and girls [to] provide for a two or three years' course of technical, commercial or domestic arts training'. The other form of school was the technical school, which could lead to tertiary study in the School of Mines. Figure 1 shows the configuration of these schools in South Australia according to a 'conspectus' provided by Schulz.

The conspectuses such as the one shown in Figure 1 acted not just as administrative maps, but also as a teleology of a socially efficient system, selecting and directing future citizens into the field for which they were 'fit'. However, it must be remembered that the processes for doing this were actually deployed with very small numbers of students, which fitted with the logic of Social Efficiency as being about the training of the most 'able'. As Figure 1 shows, with a population of over half a million in 1924, South Australia had only 24 high schools, nine Central Schools and extension classes in 19 primary schools – a tiny proportion of the whole population of 12–15-year-olds was affected. It was the emergence of new forms of educational psychology, to be discussed below, that provided the human technologies to extend to much larger populations the process of fitting young people to their future.

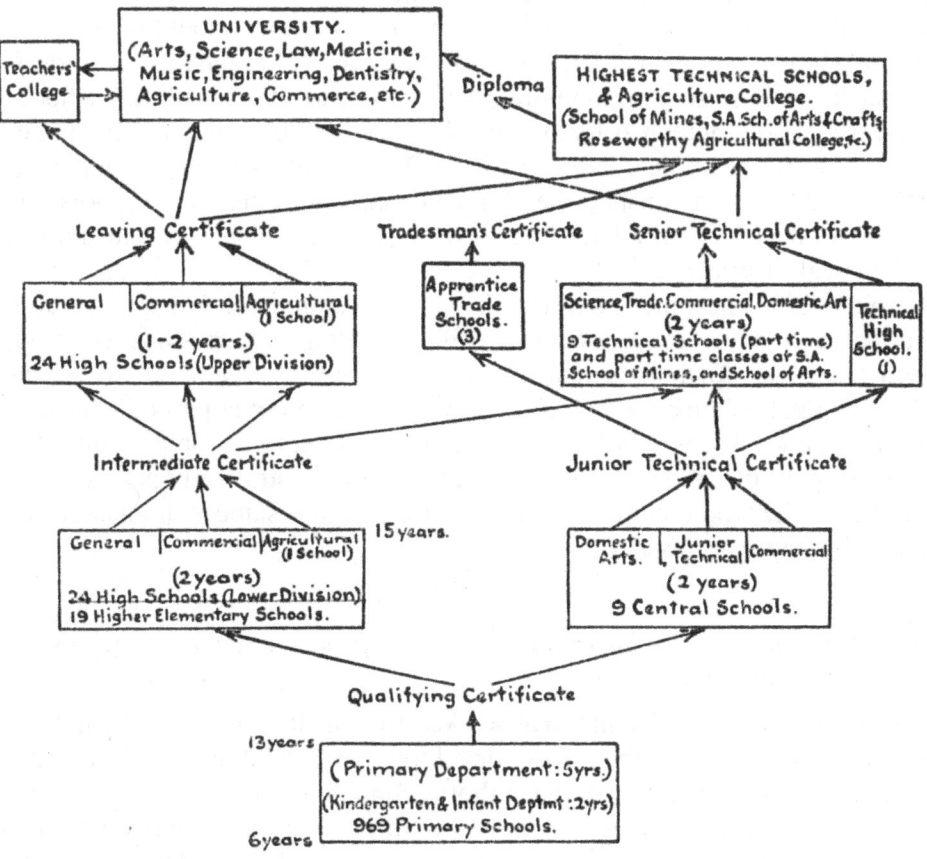

Figure 1. The conspectus for South Australian education (Schulz 1927, p. 182).

One of the key challenges identified by the authors was that of the management of populations over large distances. For example, across the chapters, the reach of post-primary schooling to the rural child was a concern, given the small numbers that might be available to form classes. For this reason, primary school extensions were an obvious solution by allowing students to stay on at primary school for a year or two, at least in the larger rural towns. In NSW, these were called Superior Schools and Cole (1927) described their reorganisation before the war as a significant step:

> They became, in effect, day continuation schools at which a broad vocational education of various types was offered. While this was being effected, however, it was necessary that they should not lead merely to a dead end. Further progress must be encouraged; and care was taken to link the Superior Public Schools with higher educational institutions. They were vocational; but they were rounded into the form of a rung on the educational ladder. (p. 40)

The concept of an 'educational ladder' referred to by Cole, common in education since the nineteenth century, was strongly promoted so that the brightest pupils (boys) could proceed all the way to the university or to specialist training such as the Teachers' College. For those who would not or could not make it all the way to the top of the ladder, there was an array of alternative school forms to the academic high school, including technical schools, agricultural schools or 'central' schools, which offered specialist streams in commerce or domestic arts. As in the example shown in Figure 1, this ladder was laid out in great detail in educational conspectuses for each state, with different schools linked by preferred pathways, all leading in theory, if not in fact, to the university or technical institutes.

Social Efficiency provided a logic that articulated schooling structures to national aspirations and a model of pathways along which students could be fitted according to their 'talent'. However, it was never about managing a whole population, only its most able. It was, therefore, only part of an ensemble of programmes that would lead secondary schooling to encompass all 12–15-year-olds possible. What it did provide was an administrative logic which could encompass the whole child population across large distances, harnessed in the name of a national project.

'Broaden the pupils' cultural outlook, develop their character and taste': the development of Culture

The second social programme that worked to constitute the reforms discussed by these educators was that of the development of 'Culture'. This was a key term in each of the chapters as the authors sought to define the nature of the curriculum that would best meet the 'needs' of this new population in post-primary schools. As Browne (1927b) put it when discussing the population of students who made up the so-called 12–15 problem:

Their future occupations will lie in commerce, arts and crafts, trade, factory work and unskilled labour. What is the most suitable curriculum for them? This is a vital question, for these scholars represent the large majority of our boys and girls. The professional course given in the high schools is unsuitable – what is required is *a curriculum with a cultural basis but a vocational bias.* (pp. 106–107, emphasis added)

The concept of a 'cultural' basis for the curriculum (Selleck 1982) hailed the key discourse of nineteenth-century education, which was that of a 'Liberal Education'. Liberal Education was dominated by debates during the nineteenth century about whether the classics or science was the better means of providing a 'general education' to the future gentlemen, clerics and leaders of society and, in the end, both were deemed important routes to the knowledge of most worth. By the twentieth century in Australia, the classics of Latin and ancient Greek were largely being replaced by literary studies in the vernacular – that is, English – which had the advantage of making it accessible to a mass child population. The study of English literature met the need in Liberal Education for a centrally educative subject which would adequately train and moralise its pupils. Matthew Arnold, a major figure in curriculum debates in England during the nineteenth century, argued that science was not a suitable subject to take a central role in a Liberal Education because it could not provide the basis for moralising students. Instead, Arnold argued for the importance of English literature as a basis for this work (Mathieson 1975). The concept of Culture, as a central moralising force, acted as a kind of counter-discourse to that of Social Efficiency in debates about educating the adolescent. During the nineteenth century, science had been finally recognised as part of a Liberal Education and as an important source of truth, but something that needed to be balanced with the moral guidance of the classics: now, in the early twentieth century, the 'vocational bias' needed for socially efficient training required 'cultural' subjects as a counterbalance.

Each of the four authors being examined here emphasised the importance of Culture within the new forms of schooling for the problem 12–15 population, to ensure that they formed appropriate and moral character habits to take them into the 'after' life (that is, after leaving school as a working citizen), as in this description of the new central schools by Clubb (1927):

While fully recognizing in the case of the boys and girls who attend the handicraft classes that specialization is not only desirable but also necessary, the syllabus has laid special stress upon the cultural subjects that will help to develop in the pupils the side of their education that means so much in after life, apart from the mere learning of a livelihood. (p. 349)

These 'cultural subjects' were the traditional subjects of the primary school, led by English (Green and Reid 2002, Green and Cormack 2008). According to Clubb (1927, p. 346), the 'purely cultural subjects [were] English Language,

Composition and Literature, History, Geography, Mathematics and Science'. These were to be supplemented by Civics, Hygiene and Physical Training in order to meet the 'real needs of the adolescent' (p. 346). For Schulz in South Australia, the new schools for 12–15-year-olds provided a 'distinctly practical training', but the schools also 'seek to broaden the pupils' cultural outlook, develop their character and taste, and strengthen their bodies' (p. 201). An examination of the South Australian Courses of Instruction produced for these new schools in the 1920s shows that English was the leading subject with the greatest allocation of time in all of them (Cormack and Green 2005). While literature was not totally dominant in the English course, as it was in the high school syllabus, reading of stories and good books remained, supplemented by a more vocational emphasis on writing, spelling and clear speech.

Thus, vocational training, the building of citizenship and the development of healthy bodies – things required in the name of a 'fit' race and an 'efficient' education system – were at all times connected to the traditional goals of moral formation via Culture. This is, perhaps, a not uncommon feature of educational discourse, where little is discarded when new goals are added to the purposes of schools. Such an articulation was best exemplified by Clubb (1927), who managed to combine the need for cultural standards with a call to greater competitiveness (Social Efficiency) and racial fitness when describing the 12–15 problem:

> The social, political and industrial conditions of to-day demand greater fitness in the individual if we are to survive in competition with other great peoples – a people with a low level of intellectual, physical, or moral development is doomed to take a subordinate place. Cultural standards – not merely book-cultural standards – must be raised, not for the few, but for the mass of the people. (p. 345)

Educational Psychology and the promise of science

A third ensemble of ideas that could be connected to thinking about the education of adolescents in *Education in Australia* was that of Educational Psychology. This was a discourse that was emergent at the time of the writing of the book and it was, therefore, much less explicitly connected to the 12–15 problem than Social Efficiency and Culture; however, it is included here because it is instructive to consider the 'surfaces of emergence' (Foucault 1972, pp. 41–42) of Educational Psychology within Australian education. As McCallum (1986, 1990) has shown, Educational Psychology was to provide, during the 1930s, a set of techniques for selecting and distributing post-primary children into the few places then available in state secondary schools. As he notes, the need to select students on the basis of 'talent', rather than of class, led to the legitimisation of psychology as central to educational provision that took account of 'individual difference' (1986, p. 231).

Psychology is mentioned by each of the four authors examined in *Education in Australia*, and the use of tests and the provision of psychological services for 'backward' or 'mentally defective' children, as Browne (1927a, p. 132) described them, were a focus, as were the development and standardisation of 'intelligence tests' across the whole population of students. Both Cole (NSW) and Browne (Victoria) discuss the standardisation of intelligence tests involving newly formed psychology sections of their respective Teachers' Colleges. Rose (1999) notes that such tests were developed during World War I for military selection and training and provided new and cheap technologies for sorting and selecting individuals.

Two key Educational Psychology constructions – normal distribution and mental capacity (usually represented as an IQ) – began to be used in relation to the adolescent during the later war years – indeed Cole (1927, p. 132) highlights that Victoria was 'early in the field with Intelligence Tests, and, by 1913, had established "tutorial" or "opportunity" classes, whereby, in a big school, backward children and those who were in some slight measure mentally defective were segregated and given special instruction'. My own study of the South Australian education scene showed that Educational Psychology became prominent in the 1920s (Cormack 2004) and quickly moved beyond its initial focus on the 'defective' child to sorting populations and being used as a basis of selection and prediction of a child's skills in the 'after [school] life'. The educational psychology sections of Teachers' Colleges and the psychology branches of the various education departments quickly moved to the use of the science in the field of vocational education. For example, in a 1925 'Talk to Teachers', the South Australian Education Department's first psychologist, Constance Davey (1925), asserted that charting the correlation between chronological, mental and school ages:

> shows the teacher of what the child is capable, and where to begin his studies. But more important than this is the fact that we can now plan his education, for we can calculate his final mental age and his rate of growth mentally. (p. 195)

And in a later article (Education Department of South Australia 1929, p. 291), which glossed the work of a Swiss psychologist Clarapède, psychology was claimed to distinguish the ideal from the 'lazy, disorderly or vicious' worker in the adolescent's character.

In Educational Psychology, there was an especially close relationship between the ideas that were used to constitute the child subject (mental capacity and the concept of talent which featured strongly in the discourse of Social Efficiency) and the technologies that were deployed in measuring and sorting actual student bodies. The surfaces of emergence of the child of Educational Psychology were pre-eminently technical and involved the incorporation of ideas that had been available for some time from Child Study (Reid 1996), notably the work of G. Stanley Hall, such as stages of development, and from primary schooling (such as age-grading), into new technologies of normal distribution and mental (or IQ) testing. Interestingly, in describing the standardisation of group intelligence tests with 6000 NSW children, Cole (1927, p. 62) noted that '[i]n order to exclude the social factor, equal numbers were taken from areas of each of the following types – low grade social, middle grade social, high grade social', mirroring almost exactly the tripartite forms of school structure his chapter describes for the post-primary child – high school for the university bound, technical schools for the middle professions and terminal forms of schooling for those who would move into homes (girls), factories or farms. As Rose (1999) puts it, in the psychological sciences:

> frequently the norms that enable their objects to become visualized and inscribed become part of the scientific perception as a consequence of having first been part of a social and institutional programme of regulation – and to such programs they are destined to return. (p. 137)

The major authorities in Educational Psychology for Australian educators were Cyril Burt from England and, to a lesser extent, Lewis Terman from the USA. Each of these men was pre-eminent in his country at that time in issues of Educational Psychology. Terman worked on refinements to the IQ test and was originally a student of Hall. In South Australia, Burt had a number of articles and talks reproduced or extracted for teachers by the Education Department during the 1920s and was quoted in articles written by Davey. Both Terman and Burt were also leading figures in the eugenics movement, which saw feeble-mindedness as a threat to the health of the race and sought ways to identify and deal with it to prevent degeneration (Rose 1999, pp. 139–143). The association with the eugenics movement also maintained the racial foundations of developmental stages established by Hall.

Across the four chapters, there is a strong faith in the promise of psychology as a science to lead to progress in the identification and management of problem populations, including 12–15-year-olds who were not destined for university. The psychology of the time was strongly connected to racial ideals, via eugenics, expressed in both the book's introduction and some of the chapters. Educational Psychology was also connected with Social Efficiency through its ability to identify educational futures as connected with 'talent' or 'individual difference' rather than with class, although, as we have seen, the structures of schooling and class provided a frame for their constitution.

Conclusion

This examination of *Education in Australia*, which was published in 1927 and authored by educators at the peak of their field at the time, has provided a unique insight into a field of universal adolescent schooling in the period of its formation. Through the lens of the '12–15 problem', we see the way that a new population could be formed as an object of schooling and as subjects to carry the fears and aspirations of a white, isolated, 'British' nation in the south. As it turned out, the incorporation of the whole of the 12–15-year-old population into schooling was not actually realised until after World War II and, indeed, provision for their schooling was reduced during the Great Depression (McCallum 1986).

I have argued that the development of universal schooling for children of this age was not a singular project of reform but the consequence of a range of disparate programmes, ideals, discourses and techniques – a *dispositif* – that, nevertheless, came to form a governmental programme that came to fruition at the close of World War II and which has expanded to the present day. *Education in Australia* provides a useful lens for seeing the way these different elements could be articulated, and used to shape an enduring social programme, while also showing the fragile and 'made-up' character of the process.

One of the large shadows this history casts on the present day in education is the significance of racial discourse in the establishment of mass education for the post-primary child in Australia. I have argued that the establishment of post-primary schooling should be seen as part of a larger process of constituting the whole population of young people after primary school who had formerly been excluded from school – the working class, the isolated, the 'physically afflicted' and the 'mentally defective' – as educable.

What made this incorporation of problem populations urgent, and therefore possible as a national project, were a fear of racial decline and the urgency of building the competitiveness of the nation and empire. Social Efficiency offered the administrative logics for designing the educational pathways, managed across space and time, for directing youth to the work for which they were best fitted. Science, in the form of Educational Psychology, offered the technologies that could array these populations of young people on grids that could direct these young people into schools and curricula appropriate to their needs and specify appropriate destinations for their 'after life'. An older discourse of Culture, via a 'liberal education', offered the hope of moralising these problem populations.

In time, racial and eugenic ideals of 'fitness' and mental 'hygiene' would become less strident and, in Bessant's terms, 'more covert', but the actual practices of selection and specification of schooling through class- and ability-based categorisations would be built into the core of post-primary schooling and remain firm pillars of their organisation and results to this day (Teese 2000, Teese and Polesel 2003). In the present, new discourses shape educational ideals and the technologies used to define and shape populations in and through schooling. However, continuities with the 1920s remain. Neo-liberal modes of managing populations through shaping citizens as 'entrepreneurial selves' (Kelly 2006) still rely on discourses of competition and risk. Science, too, through standardised forms of assessment and 'evidence-based' practices, continues to offer the promise of a more 'effective' future. And yet, the same populations are framed as problems in our schools, for now those pupils who are 'differently circumstanced and with other aims' have become students 'at risk'.

Notes
1. This heading was used in four of the six chapters, on each of the largest states by population at the time, although for the largest state of New South Wales the heading was the 'twelve to fourteen problem'.
2. For an extended discussion of the concept of dispositif, see Deleuze (1992) and Bussolini (2010). For an example of this process in relation to the teaching of English to adolescents in early twentieth-century Australia, see Cormack (2007).
3. Richardson (1994) and Baker (2004) argue that the exclusion of 'delinquents', the 'subnormal' and others into their own institutions prior to the nineteenth century made the establishment of compulsory schooling possible. Richardson traces the way that the formalisation of the Special Education category in the USA from the mid-nineteenth century and the management of problem subjects within the purview of the school were made thinkable by a turn away from institutional confinement to more 'caring' discourses of prevention and rehabilitation as the state took a more 'paternal' role in the health of the citizenry. I argue that there is a continuity here with the move to bring the whole population of older children, or adolescents, into schooling.

References

Baker, B., 2001. *In perpetual motion: theories of power, educational history and the child*. New York: Peter Lang.
Baker, B., 2004. The functional liminality of the not-dead-yet-students, or, how public schooling became compulsory: a glancing history. *Rethinking history*, 8 (1), 5–49.
Bessant, J., 1991. Described, measured and labelled: eugenics, youth policy and moral panic in Victoria in the 1950s. *In*: R. White and B. Wilson, eds. *For your own good: young people and state intervention in Australia (Journal of Australian Studies Special Issue)*. Bundoora: La Trobe University, 8–28.
Blake, L.J., ed., 1973. *Vision and realisation: a centenary history of state education in Victoria*. Vol. 1. Melbourne: Education Department of Victoria.
Browne, G.S., 1927a. Educational statistics relating to the six states of Australia. *In*: G.S. Browne, ed. *Education in Australia: a comparative study of the educational systems of six Australian states*. London: Macmillan, 418–461.
Browne, G.S., 1927b. Introduction. *In*: G.S. Browne, ed. *Education in Australia: a comparative study of the educational systems of six Australian states*. London: Macmillan, xvii–xxi.
Browne, G.S., 1927c. Victoria. *In*: G.S. Browne, ed. *Education in Australia: a comparative study of the educational systems of six Australian states*. London: Macmillan, 82–170.
Browne, G.S., ed., 1927d. *Education in Australia: a comparative study of the educational systems of six Australian states*. London: Macmillan.

Bussolini, J., 2010. What is a dispositive? *Foucault studies*, 10 (November), 85–107.
Campbell, C., 1995. Secondary schooling, modern adolescence and the reconstitution of the middle class. *History of education review*, 24 (1), 53–73.
Campbell, C., Hooper, C., and Fearnley-Sander, M., 1999. *Toward the state high school in Australia: social histories of state secondary schooling in Victoria, Tasmania and South Australia*. Vol. 1. Sydney: Australian and New Zealand History of Education Society.
Carnegie Council on Adolescent Development, 1989. *Turning points: preparing American youth for the 21st century*. Washington, DC: Carnegie Corporation of New York.
Clubb, W., 1927. Western Australia. *In*: G.S. Browne, ed. *Education in Australia: a comparative study of the educational systems of six Australian states*. London: Macmillan, 314–384.
Cole, P.R., 1927. New South Wales. *In*: G.S. Browne, ed. *Education in Australia: a comparative study of the educational systems of six Australian states*. London: Macmillan, 1–81.
Cole, P.R., ed., 1935. *The education of the adolescent in Australia*. Vol. 32. Melbourne: Melbourne University Press.
Consultative Committee of the Board of Education, 1927. *The education of the adolescent: report of the Consultative Committee (Hadow Report)*. London: Board of Education.
Cormack, P., 2004. *Adolescence, schooling and English/literacy: formations of a problem in early twentieth century South Australia*. Thesis (PhD). University of South Australia.
Cormack, P., 2007. *English curriculum as dispositif: constituting adolescence in a school subject*. Paper presented at the American Educational Research Association Annual Meeting, 9–13 April, Chicago.
Cormack, P. and Green, B., 2005. *A problem subject? English/literacy, middle schooling and curriculum history*. Paper presented at the Annual Meeting of the American Educational Research Association, 10–15 April, Montreal, Canada.
Davey, C., 1925. The intellectually subnormal child and his education. *The Education Gazette*, 15 July, pp. 194–197.
Deleuze, G., 1992. What is a dispositif? (T.J. Armstrong, Trans.). *In*: T.J. Armstrong, ed. *Michel Foucault: philosopher*. New York: Harvester Wheatsheaf, 159–168.
Education Department of South Australia, 1929. Vocational guidance: testing the abilities of students. *The Education Gazette*, November, pp. 290–292.
Foucault, M., 1972. *The archaeology of knowledge and the discourse on language* (A.M.S. Smith, Trans.). New York: Pantheon Books.
Foucault, M., 1991. Questions of method. *In*: G. Burchell, C. Gordon, and P. Miller, eds. *The Foucault effect: studies in governmentality*. Chicago, IL: University of Chicago Press, 73–86.
Green, B., 2005. Post-curriculum history? *In*: C. Marsh, ed. *Curriculum controversies: point and counterpoint 1980–2005*. Deakin West, ACT: Australian Curriculum Studies Association, 115–119.
Green, B. and Cormack, P., 2008. Curriculum history, 'English' and the new education; or, installing the empire of English? *Pedagogy, culture and society*, 16 (3), 253–267.
Green, B. and Reid, J.-A., 2002. Constructing the teacher and schooling the nation. *History of education review*, 31 (2), 30–44.
Hall, G.S., 1904. *Adolescence: its psychology and its relations to physiology, anthropology, sociology, sex, crime, religion and education*. Vols. 1 and 2. New York: D. Appleton and Company.

Hansen, M.P., 1923. *Report of the Chief Inspector of secondary schools: on educational systems and administration and especially on secondary and continued education in England and America*. Melbourne: Education Department, Victoria.

Kelly, P., 2006. The entrepreneurial self and 'youth at-risk': exploring the horizons of identity in the twenty-first century. *Journal of youth studies*, 9 (1), 17–32.

Kliebard, H.M., 1995. *The struggle for the American curriculum 1893–1958*. New York: Routledge.

Lesko, N., 2001. *Act your age: a cultural construction of adolescence*. New York: Routledge Falmer.

Lovell, H.T., 1935. Psychological and social characteristics of adolescence. *In*: P.R. Cole, ed. *The education of the adolescent in Australia*. Melbourne: Melbourne University Press, 48–86.

Mathieson, M., 1975. *The preachers of culture: a study of English and its teachers*. Totowa, NJ: Rowman and Littlefield.

McCallum, D., 1986. Educational expansion, curriculum reform and psychological theory: Australia in the 1930s. *The Australian & New Zealand journal of sociology*, 22 (2), 225–237.

McCallum, D., 1990. *The social production of merit: education, psychology, and politics in Australia, 1900–1950*. London and New York: Falmer.

Mosely Educational Commission, 1904. *Reports of the Mosely Educational Commission to the United States of America, October–December 1903*. London: Cooperative Printing Society.

Reid, J.-A., 1996. Holding firm the bonds of convention: primary English, child study and the 'competent teacher'. *Changing English*, 6 (2), 197–218.

Richardson, J.G., 1994. Common, delinquent, and special: on the formalization of common schooling in the American states. *American educational research journal*, 31 (4), 695–723.

Rose, N., 1999. *Governing the soul: the shaping of the private self*. London: Free Association Books.

Samson, P.G., 1925. *A comparison of Scottish and Victorian education, shewing in particular that Victoria can derive much benefit from a study of the type of education given in Scottish schools between the ages of twelve and fifteen*. Thesis (MEd). University of Melbourne.

Schulz, A.J., 1927. South Australia. *In*: G.S. Browne, ed. *Education in Australia: a comparative study of the educational systems of six Australian states*. London: Macmillan, 171–238.

Selleck, R.J.W., 1982. State education and culture. *Australian cultural history*, 1 (1), 29–42.

Teese, R., 2000. *Academic success and social power: examinations and inequality*. Carlton South: Melbourne University Press.

Teese, R. and Polesel, J., 2003. *Undemocratic schooling: equity and quality in mass secondary education in Australia*. Carlton: Melbourne University Press.

Williams, A., 1908. *Preliminary report of the Director of Education upon observations made during an official visit to Europe and America, 1907*. Adelaide: South Australian Government.

'To see through Johnny and to see Johnny through': the guidance movement in interwar Australia

Katie Wright

Melbourne Graduate School of Education, The University of Melbourne, Melbourne, Australia

> In the late 1920s and early 1930s, the guidance movement secured a foothold in the Australian educational landscape. Educators and psychologists looked to new initiatives in Britain and America in the hope that guidance programmes would provide solutions to a range of social, economic and educational problems: vocational guidance to help young people identify their calling and secure employment, educational guidance to assist with post-primary selection and placement, and child guidance clinics for the treatment of emotional, psychological and behavioural problems. The distinctive aims of different forms of guidance, however, have tended to obscure in recent historiography the common ideas and rationales that underpinned their establishment: in short, the preclusion of social, educational and industrial 'misfits'. This article argues, therefore, for a reconceptualisation of guidance as a broader philosophy of individualised education, with a related set of practices, that took root internationally during the interwar years. Through a focus on developments in Australia, an examination of guidance in this broader sense points to the critical place of psychological knowledge and the expanding role of schools in managing the development of children and adolescents and guiding them towards adulthood and future citizenship.

Introduction

First, what is meant by the 'guidance movement'? The reader doubtless knows the old definition, 'Guidance is the effort to see through Johnny and to see Johnny through'. The more recent statement, 'Guidance is the effort to help Johnny see through himself and to see himself through', is proof of developing insight into a sound underlying philosophy ... (Sarah Sturtevant 1937, p. 347)

In 1937, Sarah Sturtevant of Teachers' College, Columbia University, published something of a stocktake of the guidance movement in the USA. She catalogued a range of activities which, she argued, had enabled the visionary ideal of individualised education to shift from a position of relative obscurity to 'a place in the educational sun' (Sturtevant 1937, p. 346). Amongst the examples she cited of fitting a person's education to his or her individual needs were the establishment of guidance services, intelligence testing and new approaches to character education. The advancement of scientific knowledges was providing, she noted, new insights into human development. The work of nutritionists and biologists had thrown light on the physical bases of behaviour, while psychologists were generating new insights into 'the laws of learning' and individual differences. Such developments made possible the kinds of individualised educational approaches that Sturtevant and others of this time broadly referred to as 'guidance'.

Several years later, C. Gilbert Wrenn (1940), Professor of Educational Psychology at the University of Minnesota, described guidance as a 'personalizing influence in the life of a child' (p. 176). Wrenn (1940) noted that much confusion had arisen because the term guidance referred to the provision of specialised services for students, as well as 'a point of view which affects all of the educational programs' (p. 175). As Wrenn explained, the so-called guidance outlook encompassed diverse concerns with character, personality and behaviour. As such, it was an emerging educational philosophy that its proponents hoped would increasingly shape curriculum content, pedagogical practices and the organisation of schooling more generally (Brewer 1937, Wrenn 1940, Faulkner 1941). But guidance, as it is more commonly understood in the present, also referred to a quite distinct set of specialised practices, and it was in the development of these activities that the ideal of individualised education, as articulated by Sturtevant and her contemporaries, was perhaps most strikingly manifest: educational guidance to assist pupils to choose appropriate courses of study, vocational guidance to help with the choosing of a suitable career and child guidance to help the 'emotionally maladjusted' (Sturtevant 1937, p. 346).

Within the broader context of the progressive education movement and international, notably American, discussions about guidance and the individualising of education (Adams 1973), I explore in this article key manifestations of the guidance movement during the interwar years in Australia. In describing Australian developments, however, I use the term 'guidance movement' advisedly. Comparisons with the USA and indeed with Britain might suggest little by way of a widespread movement in Australia at this time – if a tally of guidance services was taken as the primary measure. Yet I argue, as Sturtevant and others might, that it was a movement characterised as much by new ideas and shifting philosophies of education as it was by the emergence of new programmes of student support. The prominence of vocational guidance, moreover, has tended to overshadow, historically, broader notions of guidance and the interconnections between the different forms it took. As such, I argue that it is fruitful to revisit this more inclusive conceptualisation of guidance – as both an educational philosophy and a related set of practices – that so exercised American educators in the 1930s. This line of enquiry situates services, or 'procedures', as Wrenn (1940) referred to guidance programmes, within a broader frame of educational developments and, in doing so, throws light on both the sphere of practice and the broader realm of educational ideas. Tracing early developments in this domain provides, I argue, productive insights into the increasing importance of psychology in education and the expanding role of schools in managing the development of children and adolescents and guiding them towards future citizenship.

To explore this, I begin by examining the influence of the 'new psychology' on Australian education during the 1920s and 1930s within the broader social context of rising concern about 'misfits'. Informed by genealogical approaches, I situate the introduction of guidance services not only as the realisation of a visionary educational ideal, but also as a practical response to emergent social issues, notably those associated with the expansion of post-primary schooling, youth unemployment and concerns about mental hygiene. I then examine the establishment of vocational guidance, educational guidance and child guidance services in Australia, illustrating some of the precipitating factors and institutional arrangements in which such practices arose. In the final section of the article, I argue that while guidance activities were still nascent in Australia during the interwar years, the influence of what the Americans called a 'guidance outlook' was evident in the broader realm of ideas. This overarching philosophy of the guidance movement, I suggest, was shaping not only specialised guidance services, but also broader educational reforms, evident in such practices as intelligence testing and ability grouping.

Psychology, guidance and the problem of 'misfits'

During the early decades of the twentieth century, the growth of psychology as a discipline and its practical application in educational settings laid the basis for a new conceptualisation of the self, one in which the developing child was increasingly understood as comprehensible and calculable and was in turn subject to new forms of classification (McCallum 1990, Rose 1999, Wright 2011). This had a profound impact on the educational enterprise in Australia, as it did in other parts of the Western world. The ways in which psychology was shaping education during this time, and indeed the ways in which perceived educational problems were in turn shaping directions in psychology, are clearly beyond the scope of this article. What is important to acknowledge here, however, is the critical role of psychology in the emergence of the guidance movement and more generally in the kinds of child-centred approaches that were characteristic of the progressive philosophies of New Education in the early twentieth century (Jenkins 2000).

At the 1923 meeting of the Australasian Association for the Advancement of Science, J.A. Johnson (1924), Principal of the Teachers' Training College in Hobart, described psychology as giving rise to something of an educational revolution, as the 'new psychology' was received in Australia with 'extraordinary fervour' (p. 698). In his presidential address for Section J: Mental Science and Education, he described the 'old psychology' as one that sought by means of mental introspection an understanding of the soul and its destiny. In doing so, it emphasised cognition and was primarily concerned with normality. By contrast, the 'new psychology', he argued, sought to understand emotional life and behaviour and, critically, was far more cognisant of abnormality. Developments in psychology had, Johnson (1924) asserted, presented not only a speculative interest, but also an interest that was 'materially changing the educational outlook' (p. 697).

By the 1920s, there was considerable enthusiasm about the promise of psychology in tackling pressing social and economic issues. The popular press regularly reported on public lectures and meetings of learned societies and social organisations where new ideas about psychology and its social utility were canvassed. A key focus of this attention centred on the practical application of psychology in schools abroad, particularly in America and England, and specifically on the value of intelligence testing. A 1921 article in the *West Australian*, for example, declared that the 'application of mental tests to determine the mental levels of individual pupils with a view to their more scientific classification is one of the outstanding features of American education' (Miles 1921, p. 22). With its capacity to measure intelligence, the new psychology provided a scientific basis for the classification of individual differences, which in turn brought the ideal of individualised education into closer reach.

The reporting of international education practices in the popular press and in professional publications reflected a keen interest of Australian educators in developments abroad. While Australian educational systems had been principally shaped by British tradition, by the late 1920s there was increasing interest in American education (Cunningham 1930a). Through international study tours of education systems and through participation in international conferences, new techniques and emerging models of practices were documented (see, for example, Parker 1935). As K.S. Cunningham, founding director of the Australian Council for Educational Research (ACER), noted in 1930: 'Australia will undoubtedly continue to develop her own educational systems in her own ways'. However, he pointed out that in some important respects, 'Australian conditions, problems and points of view are more akin to those of the United States than to those of England' (Cunningham 1930a, p. 10). In addition to his comparison of administrative problems in the United States and Australia, Cunningham also discussed various other aspects of school life, including psychological examinations. He reported favourably on the widespread use of intelligence testing in the USA and suggested that, 'on the whole, Australian educational practice is backward in making any extensive use of such tests' (Cunningham 1930b, p. 40).

Cunningham's critique notwithstanding, the application of the new psychology in the form of the mental testing of school children occurred quite early in Australia (Turtle 1988). Australian interest in testing reflected broader international enthusiasm, which coincided with the expansion of mass schooling throughout Europe and the USA (Down 2001). Soon after the publication of Binet's first scale of intelligence in 1905, and his revised versions of 1908 and 1911, R.G. Cameron (1913) and Elizabeth Skillen (1913) of the Sydney Teachers' College had both published Australian test results, with Skillen using her own revision of the Binet scale. Certainly, the mental testing of school children during the 1920s and 1930s across most Australian states remained limited. However, important developments were occurring, particularly in New South Wales (NSW) and Victoria. In 1923, a psychological laboratory was established at the Melbourne Teachers' College, with Cunningham in charge (Lewis 1987). It provided an important institutional base for the advancement of experimental psychology in general and for mental testing in particular, spreading what Lewis (1987, p. 154) refers to as 'an ideology of individual differences based on a concept of intelligence that was measurable, fixed and inherited'. With a demonstrable capacity to measure intelligence, the psychological laboratory also played an important role in Victoria in the establishment of special schools and opportunity classes for the children deemed to be 'mentally deficient'.

The broader social context for the enthusiastic embrace of the psychometric techniques of the new psychology was widespread concern about 'feeblemindedness' and a growing interest in child study and individual differences (McCallum 1990). In the 1920s, psychologists were appointed to Education Departments in a number of Australian states and measures of intelligence were increasingly used for the purposes of classification and educational placement, particularly of children identified as 'different' (Turtle 1988, p. 233). In an address on individual differences to the Legacy Club in Melbourne in 1925, Cunningham referred to a major problem of modern education being 'to make educational facilities fit the ability of all children'. He went on to say that with the aid of 'differential psychology', it would 'eventually be possible to fit every child for the work for which he was best fitted and thereby avoid the "misfits" of later life' (Argus 1925, p. 8).

Concern about 'misfits' loomed large in the social imaginary and in many ways constituted the problem that guidance was invented to solve. It was in this context that Australian educators and psychologists sought to emulate British and American programmes of guidance, initiatives that held the promise of solutions to a range of social, economic and educational problems. There was much enthusiasm about what might be achieved with the introduction of such methods, as this excerpt from a *Sydney Morning Herald* article illustrates:

> Australia to-day is full of social and industrial misfits, and while ever this position remains we must always expect dread and industrial strife, social unrest, and

economic failure ... This 'round peg in a square hole' evil is one that is rapidly assuming large proportions and it is the duty of every nation ... to eradicate it. The remedy is simple. As each child leaves school he or she should be examined by a trained industrial psychologist to find the most suitable vocation ... The science of character analysis and scientific vocational advice is going to play a big part in the industrial and social welfare of the world. (Eureka 1928, p. 10)

Psychological guidance offered a way of tackling the apparently escalating problem of the so-called educational misfits and industrial misfits and the even more intractable problem of social misfits. Early intervention and expert assistance could, it was argued, prevent the development of misfits in schools, in work and in life. Vocational guidance promised to be an effective means of steering young people towards suitable careers and educational guidance an efficient and effective way of managing post-primary selection and placement, while child guidance could help children with social and emotional problems. What united the emancipatory promise of guidance in its various forms was the amelioration of pressing social and economic problems, as well as the prevention of future problems. It offered the hope of avoiding inefficiency by preventing young people becoming educational and occupational misfits and, in the case of child guidance, preventing maladjustment, delinquency and, ultimately, the problem of social misfits.

The establishment of guidance services in Australia

I turn now to how the aims and ideals of guidance as specialised services took institutional form in Australia. A rather obvious point perhaps but one that should be made at the outset is that vocational and educational guidance in many ways represented the formalisation of longstanding practices of teachers and others offering assistance, advice and counsel to young people. The establishment of guidance services in and outside the state schooling systems in Australia thus reflected broader processes of modernisation, the influence of international, especially American, educational practices and the growing significance of psychology. Vocational guidance and educational guidance in particular were also promoted in the interest of national efficiency. Child guidance has a somewhat different genealogy, with its heritage more closely aligning with the development of psychological medicine. However, as I will argue below, there were nevertheless important connections and thus there is strong merit in considering their commonalities. First, however, I examine the manifestation of guidance in its more prominent forms.

Vocational and educational guidance

Economic and social pressures during the early part of the twentieth century gave considerable momentum to the development of systems of vocational guidance. Processes of industrialisation, the changing nature of work and youth unemployment were important economic drivers (Sherington 1991). Coupled with this were exigent social anxieties about idle youth and emerging orthodoxies of adolescence as a turbulent and troubling time (Hall 1907, Holbrook 1989). It was within this context that steering young people into suitable vocations assumed a new urgency and Australian educators sought to establish forms of vocational guidance connected with the state schooling systems.

Not surprisingly, there was considerable interest from those charged with the preparation of boys for trades. James Nangle, Superintendent of Technical Education in NSW, for example, chose vocational guidance as the subject of his 1924 presidential address to the Mental Science and Education section of the Australasian Association for the Advancement of Science. Nangle was particularly concerned about the drift of boys leaving school at age 14 and then finding themselves unemployed soon after. In that address, he argued:

> If education is to have any real value it must be planned to produce happy and efficient citizens. It is impossible for any citizen to be either happy or efficient if forced to live a life of work in a calling for which he is fitted neither by taste nor aptitude. (Nangle 1926, p. 617)

Nangle (1926) was particularly enthusiastic about the use of psychological tests:

> Without going as far as saying that all children should be measured for intelligence and school achievement, and that all should have their vocations fixed as a result of these measurements, it can be claimed that some useful estimate of vocational fitness is practicable, and that it is possible to establish a ready passage from school to the learning of a suitable calling. In short, that most of the callings can be classified as regards the native capacity and attainment required to successfully follow them .... (p. 618)

A similar position was advanced the following year by the NSW Minister for Public Instruction. Like Nangle, he regarded vocational guidance as a preventative measure against a problem that had become all too apparent: the drifting of boys into 'dead-end' jobs. While there had already been moves to assist boys attending Junior Technical Schools to find apprenticeships, it was his view that vocational guidance should be developed further still, so that all children finishing school 'may be assisted to become self-supporting and self-reliant citizens' (NSW Department of Public Instruction 1926, p. 4). A vocational guidance bureau was subsequently established in the NSW Education Department in 1926 (NSW Department of Public Instruction 1927). During its first years of operation, the emphasis was on vocational placement. However, with the appointment of a psychologist in 1928, the work of the bureau increasingly involved mental testing and psychological analysis of skills and aptitudes (NSW Department of Public Instruction 1929). In a survey of vocational guidance across the Australian states in 1932, G.R. Giles (1932) outlined the NSW scheme:

> Boys and girls who have completed their third year in the post-primary course in the metropolitan area, or who have attained the age of 16 years, are interviewed by appointment, when they are subjected to a series of psychological tests. Vocational guidance is given on the results of these tests, which are supplemented by the information contained on the Cumulative History Cards... The card gives a record of progress in the different school subjects, of punctuality, of conduct etc.... Teachers are asked to express an opinion as to character and temperament qualities, to state whether home conditions are normal or otherwise, and to define the interest taken by the child in hobbies and sports. The child is also asked to make a first and second choice of vocation and the parent requested to express his or her desire in this connection, while the teacher is required to state his opinion as to the suitability of choice. (p. 532)

In devising models of vocational guidance, educational bureaucrats in NSW and other states made close study of international education systems. A number of people who held significant positions in Australian education returned from travels abroad much enthused by modern educational initiatives, including guidance. S.H. Smith, Director of Education in NSW, made a special investigation of vocational guidance during a study tour of Europe in 1926 (NSW Department of Public Instruction 1927). Smith's observations during that time considerably shaped the work subsequently undertaken in NSW, particularly with the introduction of Cumulative School History cards. As Giles (1932) outlined, this system involved a new kind of observation of young people, not only a detailed recording of educational progress, but also assessments of personality, emotional traits and home life (NSW Department of Public Instruction 1929).

Similarly, in Victoria, an international study tour also preceded the advent of vocational guidance in that state. In late 1926 and early 1927, the Chief Inspector of Primary Schools, James McRae, visited the USA, Britain and Europe on a travelling scholarship awarded by the Victorian Department of Education. His initial brief was to report on school administration and superintendence, but the Education Minister later commissioned him to also investigate vocational guidance (McRae 1927). As Holbrook (1989) has observed, the intense interstate rivalry between NSW and Victoria likely played an important role in this development. Indeed, Victoria's decision to investigate vocational guidance abroad occurred very soon after the establishment of the NSW bureau. McRae (1927) spent eight and a half months abroad discussing a range of educational problems with administrative and professional officers in each of the countries he visited. But of his study of education in other lands, he was later to say that nothing made a deeper impression upon him than the importance attached to vocational guidance in schools (McRae 1928).

In an article published in the *Education Gazette and Teachers' Aid* the year after he returned, McRae (1928) noted: 'Many of the delinquent practices found in adolescents are definitely acquired during the disastrous period of idleness or of drifting from one job to another that so often follows cessation of school attendance' (p. 307). He finished his plea for vocational guidance by stating:

> Let us keep in mind that vocational guidance has definitely come to stay. If we are to hold our own in competition with other lands, we must see to it that our young people are rightly informed about, and guided in their choice of, their future occupations. We must study what is being done abroad and in other Australian States, and lose no time in the adoption of methods and measures that have stood the test of trial in other school systems. It is hoped that the coming year will see a wholehearted response in our schools in this important field of educational effort. (McRae 1928, p. 308)

An especially vocal proponent of vocational guidance, McRae was instrumental in the establishment of a Victorian scheme in 1929 (Giles 1932). His enthusiasm about the potential of vocational guidance not only to remedy problems of vocational adjustment, but also for it to be part of a broad and systematic approach to education and work that would help all young people, was an enthusiasm that was widely shared. The Victorian approach was envisaged to deal with three potential problems arising from the transition from primary to post-primary school and later from school to work: choice of post-primary course, choice of suitable career and placement in chosen calling (Giles 1932). The solution to the first problem – post-primary placement – was educational guidance. Selecting a suitable course of study was deemed to be the role of teachers and parents, who would assist the child in the sixth year of school to decide broadly on his or her future working life: 'professional and commercial occupations on the one hand and industrial and rural callings on the other, with the addition, in the case of girls, of careers in home management' (Giles 1932, p. 535). Like NSW, Victoria introduced a system of record cards that would accompany young people throughout their schooling and in the immediate years that followed. These were envisaged as an important part of the vocational guidance toolkit.

The first stage of vocational guidance in Victoria was deemed to be largely 'educational in character' (Victoria 1930, p. 465). Head teachers were advised to send a circular to the parents of children in Grade VI, seeking information on likely age of school leaving, preferred occupation and any other information that might assist with educational placement. How closely teachers followed this directive is difficult to ascertain. However, a departmental reminder to head teachers of the need to 'consider the educational plans of pupils before advising the most suitable type of school for further education' suggests that the system may not have always functioned along intended lines (Victoria 1933, p. 543). The Victorian scheme illustrates that in principle, if not always in practice, educational guidance was closely related to vocational guidance and its introduction was certainly underpinned by a similar rationale. The overarching aim was the prevention of educational misfits: young people who found themselves in a course of study for which they were unsuited. In the context of limited post-primary places, it became an important part of the transition process and its value was promoted on the grounds of both the efficient operation of schools and the happiness and welfare of students.

In NSW, a comprehensive system of educational guidance had been developed by the mid-1930s. It was operationalised through the introduction of a school counsellor network, with a central plank of this scheme being mass intelligence testing (Hughes 2002). The introduction of school counsellors in NSW in 1935 followed the appointment of Harold Wyndham as the Education Department's first Research Officer. Wyndham, who was later to become Director-General of Education in that state, pursued an educational reform agenda in which psychology and guidance were critical. The grouping of pupils based on 'mental age', rather than on chronological age, he argued, was key to catering for individual differences (Hughes 2002). Measuring mental ability was thus deemed critical to realising the progressive vision of individualised education. Ability grouping promised a more efficient educational system and measuring the intelligence of every child entering high school would minimise, in his view, the problem of educational misfits. However, for mass testing to be successful, a large number of skilled testers were required. This task was to become the key responsibility of the School Counselling Service, which employed teachers with psychology qualifications, whose primary task was educational guidance and the placement of students into appropriate classes and courses of study (Hughes 2002).

In the 1930s, guidance became an especially prominent educational issue in NSW (Hughes 2002). The economic Depression and rising concerns about idle youth had thrown into sharp relief the importance of vocational guidance and of education more generally in 'preparation for work and citizenship' and as 'a panacea for social and economic ills' (Holbrook 1990, p. 135). Within this context, vocational preparation and indeed guidance in a more general sense became increasingly enmeshed with the broader aims of schooling. Giles (1932) summed up the Victorian scheme as 'essentially an educational implement, which will help the child to adjust himself to school and to society with benefit to himself and his connections, and which aims to reach every child in all parts of the state' (p. 538). By the mid-1930s in NSW, state-wide intelligence testing, pupil record cards and the introduction of school counsellors comprised the core elements of 'the new guidance approach' (Hughes 2002, p. 45). The Victorian scheme, by contrast, emphasised neither testing nor placement, which meant that it diverged significantly from the model adopted in NSW (Holbrook 1989). Most other states in Australia also had by this time, at least to some degree, formalised educational and vocational guidance services. Though using varying approaches, the guiding imperative differed little across the country. It was the successful placement of the young person into a suitable vocation that marked, as Giles said in 1932, 'the climax of the education drama' (p. 530).

In addition to Education Department services, a small number of private organisations also provided vocational guidance for young people. In 1927, the Australian Institute of Industrial Psychology (AIIP) was established in Sydney, modelled on the National Institute for Industrial Psychology in Britain (Walker 1929). Five years later, the Victorian Vocational and Child Guidance Centre, which later became simply the Victorian Vocational Guidance Centre, commenced operation (Wright 2012). There are few records remaining from the Melbourne Centre, but records from the AIIP in Sydney provide some indication of the sorts of vocational guidance reports furnished to private clients at that time. Assessments of intelligence, clerical and mechanical ability, mental speed and language were established through various psychological and aptitude tests. The reports also included a more general assessment of the young person, evident in statements such as:

> Physically he appears to be of robust constitution ... Does not exhibit any factors which are likely to preclude him from any particular occupation ... Temperamentally he is inclined to be somewhat self-conscious ... otherwise his outlook on life is healthy and normal ... In numerical calculation he is outstanding. From this we conclude that he is well fitted for a practical professional career and we would suggest engineering, architecture, or medicine, in that order of suitability.[1]

The work of the AIIP, however, was not limited to assessments of vocational suitability. For what often came to light during vocational guidance was evidence of 'personal troubles' (Hales 1936). In response to this, the AIIP instituted what was referred to as the 'Worry Clinic', which drew broadly on the principles of child guidance. Individuals would receive a general psychological examination to determine abilities, and if a 'pronounced neurosis' was identified, it was recommended that they seek psychiatric treatment. As Nora Hales (1936) of the AIIP described this work:

> The designation is well suited to the general nature of the service [of vocational guidance]. It is interesting to note that the majority of the problems presented have a vocational or educational aspect, and that the 'worry clinic' is in this way the clearing house for many of the mental cares and burdens which react so unfavourably on the smooth running of business and industrial affairs. It has just as important a contribution to make to efficiency as to the more personal matter of balance and sanity. (p. 27)

Psychometric testing was central to the approach taken by the AIIP, particularly in helping young people develop self-knowledge. Helping not only 'to see Johnny through' but also to 'see through himself', as Sturtevant (1937) described guidance, was a key aim of this work. As A.H. Martin (1930), Lecturer in Psychology at the University of Sydney and Honorary Director of the AIIP, described the psychologist's work in this area:

> Not rarely is he rewarded by the knowledge that through his advice he has helped a fellow human being to know himself and has assisted him in his task of self-development, and that thus in some measure he has rendered a distinct and unique social service. (p. 149)

One of the most striking aspects of the introduction of guidance services is the extent to which its aims, rationales and guiding principles were framed as simultaneously serving two distinct purposes: social efficiency and individual happiness. A NSW *Education Gazette* (1939) article stated that educational guidance was of 'the utmost importance not only for the efficient operation of schools but for the welfare of the boys and girls and the happiness of all concerned' (p. 118). This was also the key rationale for vocational guidance. As Rose (1999) wryly notes, the developing field of industrial psychology readily seized on this, 'apparent discovery of a fortunate coincidence between personal contentment of the worker and maximum efficiency and profitability for the boss' (p. 58). Even doctors by the 1920s were arguing that a happy worker was a productive one and that the key to contentment lay in the best match between mental equipment and work tasks (MJA 1924).

During the interwar years, vocational and educational guidance reflected a tremendous optimism about the power of emerging psychological knowledges and techniques in providing new ways of 'knowing' young people, in terms of their skills and aptitudes as well as their character and their future aspirations. But there was also a parallel move taking place with the development of child guidance. Child guidance not only provided a means of identifying individual differences and assisting young people to develop self-knowledge, but also sought to correct personal deficiencies and help the developing child or adolescent who was apparently at risk of maladjustment. The concern about the preclusion of misfits therefore was not limited to the spheres of education and work, but also traversed the personal domain.

Child guidance

By the late 1920s, there was considerable concern in Australia, as there was internationally, about problems of youth mental health, delinquency and childhood maladjustment. Importantly, the psychological knowledge and language that were shaping the articulation of this problem also purported to offer a new scientific solution: the study of problems of children and their clinical management by new experts in the field of mental hygiene. Ideas about preventative mental health initiatives and early intervention emanating from America were enthusiastically embraced in Australia, and child guidance formed a key component of a new, modern approach to mental hygiene (Berry 1929, VCMH 1931).

Child guidance was largely an initiative of the American philanthropic foundation, The Commonwealth Fund (Horn 1989). Amid growing concerns about 'mental disease' and delinquency, the foundation financed the establishment of community mental health facilities in the USA for children and adolescents exhibiting social, emotional or behavioural problems: in short, problems of 'adjustment'. From a small number of 'demonstration clinics' founded in the early 1920s, by the early 1930s, there were 35 in operation across the USA and almost twice that number a decade later (Horn 1989, p. 58). The

Commonwealth Fund also financed a similar initiative in Britain in the late 1920s: the English Mental Hygiene Program. As with activities in the USA, it involved the establishment of clinics and related activities, which included the funding of mental health training courses and financial aid for an educative agency, the Child Guidance Council (Wright 2012).

As with Australian responses to international initiatives in vocational guidance, there was considerable enthusiasm about the promise of child guidance. An article in Perth's *Western Mail* (1930), headlined 'Combating insanity: new world movement', reflected the optimism about the new approach to early intervention and preventative mental health care. It reported on a trip abroad taken by a Melbourne physician, Dr Maurice Shalit, and his eagerness to see this new scientific 'system of mental hygiene' instituted in Australia. The cornerstone of the 'movement', the article noted, was the provision of child guidance clinics. As Shalit was reported as stating:

> We owe it to our future citizens to give them a chance to grow up useful and law-abiding members of the community. This clinic idea, if established on the right lines, would save them from sinking into the lowest depths of mental degeneracy ... The specialist staff of each should at least consist of a psychologist, a psychiatrist and a social worker. The psychologist's duty is to examine the child for possible mental weakness and the psychiatrist is to treat him where necessary. The social worker visits the home of the child and studies his home life and general surroundings. All three meet in conference to devise means of dealing with the problem. (*Western Mail* 1930, p. 19)

In the early 1930s, state-based Mental Hygiene councils were established in Australia, the first in Victoria in 1930 (Wright 2012). One of its original initiatives, undertaken in association with the recently formed ACER, was a study of 'problem children in Melbourne schools', which sought to ascertain the need in Victoria for a child guidance clinic (Cunningham 1932). The investigation found that some 14% of children in the Melbourne metropolitan region were 'problem cases'. Their apparent disturbances included so-called defects of personality, conduct disorders, educational defects and, simply, bad habits (Cunningham 1932, p. 85). As a result of this study, a child guidance clinic was opened in Melbourne: the Victorian Vocational and Child Guidance Centre. Its establishment was the result of the coming together of the Vocational Guidance Association and the Victorian Council for Mental Hygiene; it was determined that there was sufficient commonality between vocational guidance and child guidance to justify bringing these two forms of guidance together into the one institution (VCMH 1931).

The establishment of the Centre reflected an ambitious aim. So confident were its founders of the need and demand for career advice and child guidance services that they envisaged it would be self-funding. Their optimism proved justified in terms of vocational guidance, but the child guidance component of the centre proved too costly to be maintained. The Victorian Education

Department was supportive of the venture, insofar as it recommended the Centre to schools, but it provided no direct financial support. It was able to operate for several years with the aid of small grants, but for child guidance to be ongoing it required fees for services. This put the service out of the reach of many. After failing to secure the financial support from the state government, its child guidance activities ceased in 1936 and it became thereafter the Victorian Vocational Guidance Centre (VCMH 1936).

Other attempts at institutionalising child guidance in Australia, however, were more successful, and not surprisingly, state support proved critical. A number of child guidance clinics were established in Australia in the 1930s, some attached to hospitals and children's courts, and even more psychological clinics were being run 'along child guidance lines' (Phillips 1946). But it was the establishment in 1936 of a child guidance clinic as part of the NSW School Medical Service, and another in that state three years later, which finally saw education, at least in NSW, fully embrace the principles of child guidance. The clinics were based on the American model, with a staff comprising a psychiatrist, a psychologist and a social worker. Child guidance clinics offered a new multidisciplinary team approach to the treatment of problems of 'adjustment' in children and adolescents. Cases were referred from schools through teachers and inspectors, also from the Child Welfare Department, the children's courts and through the Research Officer and the NSW School Counselling Service (Burton 1939, Cunningham and Pratt 1940).

Children referred to child guidance clinics would typically receive a medical examination, undergo psychological testing and be visited at home by a social worker. In addition, the parent or guardian would be interviewed by the psychiatrist and requests would be made to schools to provide a report on the child's academic ability, home conditions and family situation, his or her friendship group and interests. Teachers were also asked to make an assessment of the child's personality. If educational difficulties appeared to be the problem, the psychologist would administer further testing. If the child's problem was deemed to be an emotional maladjustment needing treatment, the psychiatrist would begin therapy (Burton 1939, Wright 2012).

Child guidance was both a preventative and a remedial measure. Remedial because it was directed towards problem children, but it was also preventative insofar as it worked on a model of early intervention for the prevention of serious and long-term psychological and social problems. It complemented other forms of guidance offered in NSW and reflected too the emphasis placed on psychological approaches to education reform in that state. This is strikingly evident in the provision of the three forms of guidance that comprise the focus of this article, which enabled a 'very large percentage of children to receive both vocational advice and educational guidance', followed up where necessary with an 'adjustment service' offered in child guidance clinics (Waddington *et al.* 1950, p. 59).

By the late 1930s, the value of guidance services was widely acknowledged by Australian educators, just as the limitations of existing provision were lamented. As stated in the *Review of Education in Australia, 1938*:

> The function of guidance in education is an outcome of the now universally recognized importance of the innate and acquired differences which mark one individual from another. Perhaps nothing differentiates the education of to-day more clearly from that of fifty years ago than the attempts to cater for such differences ... The acceptance of the function of guidance brings in its train questions of diagnosis and differential treatment which are by no means simple. For certain cases, at least, highly expert services are needed. There is an increasing conviction that even ordinary educational and vocational guidance needs to be in the hands of specially trained experts. Australia still has far to go in these matters. (Cunningham *et al.* 1939, pp. 209–210)

It is, of course, difficult to speak of educational developments in Australia as a whole, given the nature of state-based administration and consequently the very different approaches adopted across the country. Indeed, there were significant state differences in how the principles of guidance were put into practice during the interwar years. NSW was a very early and enthusiastic adopter, with vocational guidance established in the mid- to late 1920s, a network of school counsellors appointed in the mid-1930s, and by the late 1930s, a number of child guidance clinics also were in operation. In other states, like Queensland, vocational guidance services remained very limited and the first fully functioning child guidance clinic was not established in that state until 1959, more than 20 years after the establishment of a child guidance clinic in NSW (Williams 1967).

Individualised education and the promise of guidance

In its various forms, guidance reflected the ideal of an individualised education, one in which psychology provided the expert knowledge necessary for guiding young people towards adulthood in an increasingly complex world. The principles of guidance during much of the interwar period were captured by the maxim 'to see through Johnny and to see Johnny through' (Sturtevant 1937). Yet by the late 1930s, as Sturtevent was writing, the nexus of the psychological and educational terrains was already shifting. 'To see through Johnny and to see Johnny through' was rapidly becoming the old view of guidance. The new view involved not just the acquisition of knowledge about the child that the guidance officer could harness in rendering assistance to the young person in his or her transition to adulthood. Rather, what was emerging as the guiding imperative was for the child to develop the kind of *self*-insight and *self*-understanding that was necessary to navigate life in the modern world. According to Sturtevant, the future of guidance lay not simply in the effort 'to see through Johnny and to see Johnny through'. The real promise was in 'helping Johnny to see through himself, so that he could see himself through' (Sturtevant 1937, p. 347).

For Sturtevant and many of her contemporaries, guidance was not a practice detached from other aspects of school life. It was a 'point of view' or philosophy that should infuse all aspects of education, including curriculum content and pedagogical practice as well as specialised guidance services. Indeed, as she argued, it is 'experience wide in its ministrations' and therefore 'has to do with *all* children, not only with those who are maladjusted or exceptional' (Sturtevant 1937, p. 348). Guidance has for this reason been understood in historiographical analysis as closely aligned with progressive education (Adams 1973). Indeed, progressivism in education and related developments in psychology made possible the introduction of guidance programmes, psychometrics and a range of psychologically infused approaches during the interwar period. While it is not possible to fully consider the myriad influences at play here, organisations such as the New Education Fellowship (NEF), explored in other articles in this volume, fostered much discussion about new ideas in psychology and their potential educational application. The fifth NEF conference held in Denmark in 1929, for example, was devoted to discussions of the new psychology and the curriculum (Boyd and Mackenzie 1930).

Critically, what psychology was able to provide by this time were not only abstract ideas and theories, but techniques of practical application that were central to the realisation of individualised education, such as mental testing. The backdrop to the story of guidance is, therefore, the kinds of changes that were taking place in relation to both the innovations and new ideas in education and, concomitantly, developments in psychology, which were both mutually reinforcing and inextricably connected (Wright 2011). Formalised guidance services, particularly those interventions underpinned by psychological knowledge, aimed to provide a new, modern and scientific understanding of the individual child. The widespread acceptance of the principles of guidance in Australia, if not the attempts to institutionalise it, therefore, points to critically important educational developments during the interwar period.

Certainly, it was vocational guidance that most readily captured the imagination of Australian educationalists and in many ways became synonymous with the guidance movement. However, as I have noted, soon after schemes of vocational and educational guidance were introduced, there were moves afoot in Australia to also establish educational guidance programmes and child guidance services. This is important, I argue, because even though educational and child guidance did not have the impact that vocational guidance did, they nevertheless formed a part of a *broader* vision of individualised education and the adoption of new practices and procedures that advanced the critical role of schooling in the production of happy, efficient and well-adjusted citizens. As with vocational guidance, educational guidance and child guidance were regarded as important in the preclusion of misfits and, ultimately, the prevention of emotional, psychological and social maladjustment in adulthood.

The cornerstone of vocational guidance and educational guidance was the capacity to utilise expert psychological knowledge to throw light on individual differences, differences that if properly understood could enable the matching of the right boys and girls with the right jobs or, in the case of educational guidance, the right course of study. Child guidance, similarly, was premised upon the capacity to categorise the child and relied on normative psychological frameworks in making determinations of individual deviance or pathology. Yet, in contrast to vocational and educational guidance, what is perhaps most interesting about child guidance is the emergence of a conception of the young person not only as *knowable*, but also as *changeable*. It is a more malleable notion of subjectivity that comes into view; the problem child is envisaged as someone who can be shaped and acted upon, his or her deficiencies eradicated and his or her prospects improved, through early intervention and with the application of expert psychological knowledge.

Concluding comments

Considering different, albeit related, manifestations of the guidance movement in concert brings into sharp relief the expanding role of educational agencies in managing the social and emotional development of young people. This kind of analysis points, of course, to the critical role of those knowledges of the human sciences that Rose (1999) refers to as 'psy', most notably psychology, but also psychiatry, psychotherapy and psychoanalysis. Examining guidance as a key way in which schools increasingly assumed responsibility for the personal domain of the child and adolescent serves as a way of historicising the contemporary – and indeed increasing – concern about student wellbeing and youth mental health. Psychology in particular has been instrumental in this regard, as it was in the development of other educational practices, such as the widespread use of intelligence testing, especially in NSW, and the introduction of ability grouping.

As I have noted, British and American programmes provided important models for Australia. However, as Holbrook (1989) has documented in relation to vocational guidance, what eventuated was not simply an emulation of international practices, but the adaptation of models to suit the Australian environment, with its vast landscape and relatively small population. State-based administration also meant that approaches varied across the country and, not surprisingly, service provision was concentrated in metropolitan areas rather than in rural and regional areas. While it is important to keep these factors in mind, the more specific argument I have been making here has been in relation to the importance of reconceptualising 'guidance' as an overarching set of educational ideas with a related set of techniques or practices that were 'new' and influential during the interwar years. An examination of the establishment of guidance services offers a way of thinking, historically, not only about the construction of the 'problem child', but about the sorts of rationales that have driven the development of expert intervention in childhood, for *all children*, not just for those deemed to be struggling or identified as having problems.

Finally, the emergence of formalised guidance for children and adolescents lends itself to analyses of disciplinary discourses and the role of psychological knowledge in the ever-expanding classification and pathologisation of young people. Certainly, psychology has been central to the development of categories of normality and abnormality, and the classification of young people according to these normative frameworks forms a critical part of the story. But there is another dimension that is less often emphasised. Indeed, what is often overshadowed is the tremendous sense of optimism, or hope, that accompanied the development of these knowledges and their application – in the school and in the clinic. In its various forms, guidance embodied or reflected a new way of thinking about social and individual problems in which early intervention was regarded as critical to preventing the development of major problems of adjustment in adulthood, problems that would affect not only the individual in question, but also society more broadly. Psychological knowledge and techniques offered a means of potentially realising, therefore, what Nangle (1926) referred to as a key aim of education: the production of happy and efficient citizens.

Acknowledgements

This article draws on research conducted for 'Educating the Australian adolescent: an historical study of curriculum, student counselling and citizenship, 1930s–1970s', Australian Research Council Discovery Grant 2009–2011. The principal researchers are Julie McLeod and Katie Wright with research fellows Sari Braithwaite, Sophie Rudolph and Amy McKernan. For helpful comments and feedback on an earlier version of this article, the author wishes to thank Sean Byrne, David Goodman and Julie McLeod.

Note

1. Sir Ernest Fisk papers. Mitchell Library, State Library of NSW [MLMSS 6275/11].

References

Adams, H.J., 1973. The progressive heritage of guidance: a view from the left. *Personnel & guidance journal*, 51 (8), 531–538.

Argus, 1925. Misfits in life: how to avoid them. *Argus*, 18 February, p. 8.

Berry, R.J.A., 1929. *Report to the Edward Wilson (of the Argus) Trust on mental deficiency in the state of Victoria, with suggestions for the establishment of a child guidance clinic*. Melbourne: The Argus.

Boyd, W. and Mackenzie, M., 1930. *Towards a new education: a record and synthesis of the discussions on the new psychology and the curriculum. Fifth world conference of the New Education Fellowship, held at Elsinore, Denmark, in August, 1929*. New York: A.A. Knopf.

Brewer, J., 1937. *Education as guidance: an examination of the possibilities of a curriculum in terms of life activities, in elementary and secondary school and college*. New York: Macmillan.

Burton, N.W., 1939. The child guidance clinic. Unpublished MA thesis. The University of Sydney.

Cameron, R.G., 1913. *The measurement of intelligence: the Binet tests applied to Australian children*. Sydney: The Teachers' College, Government Printer.

Cunningham, K.S., 1930a. Comparison of administrative problems in the United States and in Australia. In K.S. Cunningham and G.E. Phillips, eds. *Some aspects of education in the United States of America, part I*. Melbourne: Melbourne University Press, 9–24.

Cunningham, K.S., 1930b. Some non-academic features of school life in U.S.A. In K.S. Cunningham and G.E. Phillips, eds. *Some aspects of education in the United States of America, part I*. Melbourne: Melbourne University Press, 36–48.

Cunningham, K.S., 1932. *Problem children in Melbourne schools*. Australian educational studies (first series). Melbourne: Melbourne University Press, 75–85.

Cunningham, K.S., McIntyre, G.A., and Radford, W.C., 1939. *Review of education in Australia, 1938*. Capetown: Melbourne University Press in association with Oxford University Press.

Cunningham, K.S. and Pratt, J.J., 1940. *Review of education in Australia, 1939*. Melbourne: Melbourne University Press in association with Oxford University Press.

Down, B., 2001. Educational science, mental testing, and the ideology of intelligence. *Critical studies in education*, 42 (1), 1–23.

Eureka, 1928. Misfits: our industrial unrest. *Sydney Morning Herald*, 15 May, p. 10.

Faulkner, D., 1941. Educational guidance principles. *The phi delta kappan*, 24 (1), 3–7.

Giles, G.R., 1932. Vocational guidance in Australia, 1932. *International labour review*, 26 (4), 530–543.

Hales, N., 1936. Sydney's worry clinic. *Rydges*, January, pp. 27–28.

Hall, G.S., 1907. *Adolescence: its psychology and its relations to physiology, anthropology, sociology, sex, crime, religion and education*. New York: Appleton.

Holbrook, A., 1989. Models for vocational guidance in Australia 1920s–1930s: American influence in conflict with British tradition. *Journal of vocational education & training*, 41 (109), 43–52.

Holbrook, A., 1990. Apathetic parents and wilful children? Vocational guidance in the 1930s. *In*: M. Theobald and R. Selleck, eds. *Family, school and state in Australian history*. Sydney: Allen and Unwin, 134–153.

Horn, M., 1989. *Before it's too late: the child guidance movement in the United States, 1922–1945*. Philadelphia, PA: Temple University Press.

Hughes, J.P., 2002. Harold Wyndham and educational reform in Australia 1925–1968. Special issue. *Education research and perspectives*, 29 (1), June.

Jenkins, C., 2000. New education and its emancipatory interests (1920–1950). *History of education*, 29 (2), 139–151.

Johnson, J.A., 1924. The new psychology and the schools. *In*: *Report of the sixteenth meeting of the Australasian Association for the Advancement of Science*. Wellington Meeting, 1923. Wellington: Government Printer, 696–703.

Lewis, J., 1987. 'So much grit in the hub of the educational machine': schools, society and the invention of measurable intelligence. *In*: B. Bessant, ed. *Mother state and her little ones: children and youth in Australia 1860s–1930s*. Melbourne: Centre for Youth and Community Studies, 140–166.

Martin, A.H., 1930. The psychological practice of vocational guidance. *Australasian journal of philosophy*, 8 (2), 135–149.

McCallum, D., 1990. *The social production of merit: education, psychology, and politics in Australia, 1900–1950*. London: Falmer Press.

McRae, J., 1927. *Report on education in other lands*. Melbourne: Education Department.

McRae, J., 1928. Vocational guidance in schools. *Education Gazette and Teachers' Aid*, 13 December, pp. 307–308.

Miles, J.A., 1921. Education in America: the psychological clinic. *West Australian*, 4 March, p. 6.

MJA, 1924. Mental hygiene in industry. *Medical journal of Australia*, December, 629–630.

Nangle, J., 1926. Vocational guidance: address by the president. *In*: *Report of the seventeenth meeting of the Australasian Association for the Advancement of Science*. Adelaide Meeting, 1924. Adelaide: Government Printer, 617–627.

NSW, 1939. Educational guidance and what it means. *The Education Gazette*, 1 May, pp. 118–119.

NSW Department of Public Instruction, 1926. *Report of the minister of public instruction for the year 1925*. Sydney: Government Printer.

NSW Department of Public Instruction, 1927. *Report of the minister of public instruction for the year 1926*. Sydney: Government Printer.

NSW Department of Public Instruction, 1929. *Report of the minister of public instruction for the year 1928*. Sydney: Government Printer.

Parker, H.T., 1935. *The background of American education: as an Australian sees it*. Educational Research Series No. 34. Melbourne: Melbourne University Press in association with Oxford University Press.

Phillips, A.R., 1946. The approach to child guidance in Victoria. *The Hospital Magazine*, April, pp. 23–26.

Rose, N., 1999. *Governing the soul: the shaping of the private self*. 2nd ed. London: Free Association Books.

Sherington, G., 1991. Vocational guidance, training and employment of youth in New South Wales: from depression to post-war boom. *Journal of Australian studies*, 15 (31), 51–64.

Skillen, E., 1913. *The measurement of intelligence: the application of some of Binet's tests at Blackfriars*. Sydney: The Teachers' College, Government Printer.

Sturtevant, S., 1937. Some questions regarding the developing guidance movement. *The school review*, 45 (5), 346–357.

Turtle, A., 1988. Education, science and the 'common weal'. *In*: R. MacLeod, ed. *The commonwealth of science: ANZAAS and the scientific enterprise in Australasia, 1888–1988*. Melbourne: Oxford University Press, 222–246.

VCMH (Victorian Council for Mental Hygiene), 1931. *First annual report 1930–1931*. Melbourne: Brown, Prior.

VCMH (Victorian Council for Mental Hygiene), 1936. *Sixth annual report 1935–1936*. Melbourne: Government Printer.

Victoria, 1930. Vocational guidance. *Education Gazette and Teachers' Aid*, 21 October, pp. 465–466.

Victoria, 1933. Educational guidance. *Education Gazette and Teachers' Aid*, 27 November, p. 543.

Waddington, D.M., Radford, W.C., and Keats, J.A., 1950. *Review of education in Australia, 1940–1948*. Melbourne: Melbourne University Press.

Walker, E.R., 1929. Some recent developments in industrial psychology. *In*: *Report of the nineteenth meeting of the Australasian Association for the Advancement of Science. Hobart Meeting, 1928.* Hobart: Government Printer, 540–542.

Western Mail, 1930. Combating insanity: new world movement. *Western Mail*, 13 March, p. 19.

Williams, C., 1967. Child guidance and psychological services in Queensland. *Applied psychology*, 16 (1), 8–11.

Wrenn, C.G., 1940. Some points of view on guidance. *The high school journal*, 23 (4), 175–177.

Wright, K., 2011. *The rise of the therapeutic society: psychological knowledge & the contradictions of cultural change*. Washington, DC: New Academia.

Wright, K., 2012. 'Help for wayward children': child guidance in 1930s Australia. *History of education review*, 41 (1), 4–19.

Educating for 'world-mindedness': cosmopolitanism, localism and schooling the adolescent citizen in interwar Australia

Julie McLeod

Melbourne Graduate School of Education, The University of Melbourne, Melbourne, Australia

> This article examines citizenship education and pedagogies for learning to be a citizen in the interwar years in Australia. These discussions bore the influence of progressive education and its emancipatory promises. Against this, I explore the 'dividing practices' of citizenship education and the ways normative descriptions of the desired cosmopolitan student-citizen simultaneously constructed a non-citizen, the problematic student excluded from recognition, in this case Aboriginal students. These arguments are developed by comparing discussions at two international educational conferences: *Education in Pacific Countries* (1936, Hawaii), also referred to as *Education of Native Races in Pacific Countries*, and the New Education Fellowship-sponsored *Education for Complete Living: The Challenge of Today* (1937, Australia). These two conferences conveyed significant differences in understandings of adolescent capacity, the relative salience of local and international contexts, and the hopeful possibilities for future education and social citizenship. Contradictory dimensions to the political and educational catch-cry of internationalism are identified in relation to the question of educability of all or some students. Preliminary questions are raised about the colonising and racialising effects of progressive education, and its privileging of cosmopolitan ideals in the education of new citizens is examined in order to begin the groundwork for a post-colonial account of progressive education.

Introduction

'No Cosmopolitans', declared a newspaper report (*The Argus 1938*, p. 2) on the 1938 annual conference of the Victorian Teachers' Union (VTU). The conference theme of education for citizenship provoked vigorous debate on how best to approach this task. One delegate, Mr R. McLellan, argued 'that a child trained to think clearly and honestly and capable of critically examining arguments was well on the way to being a good citizen'. In a similar vein, Mr J. Benjamin (Melbourne Boys [High]) opined 'that the good citizen was the citizen capable of clear and logical thought'. Asserting the distinctiveness of the Australian character, Mr K. Cromo felt that the Australian ideal of citizenship should be quite different from the 'German ideal', which he saw reflected in exhortations for young Nazis to 'bear injustices willingly and cheerfully'. Such a view was the very 'antithesis of the Australian ideal', he observed: 'The good citizen of the democratic state should be quick to resent intolerance and injustice and mentally equipped to do so'. He concluded, 'Let us produce Australians with all their bad habits and vile accents if necessary, but still Australians rather than stilted Englishmen or cosmopolitans' (*The Argus 1938*, p. 2).

Clear-thinking, social responsibility, and Australia's national identity and its place on the world stage were recurrent themes in 1930s debates about citizenship education. Then, as now, civics education was concerned both with formal education about citizenship – imparting knowledge of civic institutions and obligations – and with practical learning about the techniques and practices that distinguished the good and responsible citizen from others. Meredyth and Thomas (1999, p. 2) acknowledge this kind of division when they argue that from its beginnings in the late nineteenth century, civics education in Australia has attended to the cultivation of 'character as well as capacity'. In this article, I examine discourses about the aims and nature of citizenship education *and* practical and pedagogical techniques for learning how to be a citizen in the interwar years in Australia. In 1930s Australia these discussions bore the influence of ideas from progressive education, exemplified in child-centred and active learning approaches to curriculum and in attention to the social dimensions of schooling, often accompanied by reference to the potential of education to achieve transformative social change. But in addition to and against such an emancipatory promise, I explore the 'dividing practices' (Isin 2002, Popkewitz 2008) of citizenship education and the ways in which the normative descriptions of the desired student-citizen simultaneously constructed a non-citizen, the problematic student excluded from recognition as a future citizen.

Citizenship in this analysis is not simply a legal status but involves practices and discourses that turn some subjects into citizens and some into strangers – it is understood as an ensemble of acts that create both citizens and their others (Isin 2002). This turns from a focus on rights or denial of rights – a more familiar approach in citizenship studies – to an analysis of a more diverse array of acts of citizenship definition, a set of practices and modes of recognition of the citizen that varied across time and place and which cannot be subsumed under a simple narrative of progress towards greater and greater inclusion and tolerance. My interest here is in the way progressive education in particular, despite its inclusive and tolerant face, also and inevitably, marginalised some students. In this case, the axis of inclusion and exclusion was related to a sense of place – at the VTU conference the world-minded student could be contrasted to the nation-minded student, but in the background there was also the Indigenous student, implicitly or explicitly understood within these progressive discourses as localised in a more limiting sense. A fully post-colonial reading of progressivism is well beyond the scope of this article, but that is, nevertheless, the terrain it seeks to begin to occupy.

These arguments are developed by juxtaposing two international conferences, one held in 1936 and the other in 1937: each addressed large questions about the philosophical and instructional purposes of education, the organisation and function of formal schooling, and the education and educability of young Australians. The two conferences are *Education in Pacific Countries* (Keesing 1938), sometimes referred to as the *Education of Native Races in Pacific Countries* (Elkin 1936); and *Education for Complete Living: The Challenge of Today* (1937). The second conference, *Education for Complete Living*, was a meeting of international experts who travelled throughout the Australian states between August and September 1937. It was organised by the UK New Education Fellowship (NEF) – one of a series of NEF international conferences held since the 1920s – in conjunction with the Australian Council for Educational Research (ACER), and with substantial funding and support from the Carnegie Corporation of New York (Cunningham 1938a). *Education in Pacific Countries* was a residential conference held over a five-week period in Honolulu during July and August 1936. It was organised by the Universities of Hawaii and Yale, funded also by the Carnegie Corporation of New York and convened by Professor Felix Keesing, an anthropologist from New Zealand, who was then working at the University of Hawaii and had been previously educated at Yale.[1] Representatives from Australia attended, and the topic of the education of Aboriginal people in Australia formed part of the conference deliberations. These conferences were part of a wider movement of 'institutionalised internationalisation' (Fuchs 2004, 2007) that flourished during the inter-war years, through networks of organisations and individual experts, including educators, and the exchange of ideas at international meetings (Brehony 2004). The League of Nations and philanthropic organisations, such as the Carnegie Corporation, played pivotal roles in cultivating such transnational activities and engagements (Fuchs 2004, Lawn 2004).

Directly and indirectly, these two conferences promoted debate about the attributes of a good student, the purposes of education in the post-primary years, and what constituted responsible education towards, and for, adulthood and citizenship. Both conferences espoused the benefits of comparative and, implicitly, transnational understandings in fostering new approaches to the education of adolescents. Yet, as I discuss below, there were significant differences in how the delegates to the two conferences approached questions about adolescent capacity, the relative salience of local and international contexts, and the hopeful possibilities for future education and social citizenship. I draw out some of the contradictory dimensions of the political and educational catch-cry of internationalism, suggesting some of the ways in which it opened up vistas for some students while closing opportunities for others. And, in a preliminary way, I raise questions about the colonising and racialising effects of progressive education and its privileging of cosmopolitan ideals in the education of new citizens.

To give a sense of broader debates at the time in Australia about civics and schooling, I begin with a snapshot of advice from 1930s educators on the aims and practices of secondary school citizenship education. Two recurrent themes are highlighted: one, a focus on the political and social imperatives for internationalism and the role of schools in promoting a cosmopolitan or worldly outlook; and second, an attention to cultivating in students an independence of mind and the habit of clear-thinking. These pedagogical aspirations can be understood in broadly Foucauldian terms as rationalities for acting on and shaping the self (Foucault 1988). There was tremendous faith in the power of these two interlinked capacities to lead to new futures and for the enlightenment virtues of cosmopolitanism and reason to deliver a new type of Australian student-citizen – a new subject of modernity. I propose, however, that the alignment of worldliness with reason and clear-mindedness had damaging consequences for the education of Aboriginal students. The cosmopolitan ideal created divisions between those adolescents deemed able to realise such capacities and those deemed incapable because of being embedded in familial and kin relations that confined them to local affiliations at the very time that internationalism and its promise to free citizens from parochial connections was lauded as the prized pedagogical virtue, even an index of educability. The repeated focus on rationality and internationalism had its own shadow.

Civics education: clear-mindedness and world-mindedness

Addressing the challenge of 'educating a democracy', an article in *The Sydney Morning Herald* (1936, January 24, p. 10) announced that, 'Our concept of education is broadening, and especially noticeable is the growing realisation that our teaching must have a social or civic value'. Such matters were also on the minds of teachers. Writing in *The Teacher's Journal* in April 1937 on the topic of 'The useful citizen', Hogben (1937) determined that citizenship requires three things: 'a sense of social responsibility', a 'love of truth and freedom' and 'the power of clear thinking' (p. 138). *The Teachers' Journal* was '*A Practical aid for teachers to the Curriculum and Requirements of the Education Department of Victoria*', and throughout the 1930s its pages, like those of other education magazines and teacher journals at the time, covered many topics to do with citizenship and the attributes of the ideal student. The need for reason and clear thinking was frequently repeated. A 1936 editorial in the *Journal* on 'Education and democracy' declared that:

To those of us who believe in democracy it seems essential today to give to every child the power to think out his own problems, and to arrive at a reasoned conclusion. We must encourage the development of that spirit of free inquiry which was perhaps the greatest gift of ancient Greece to the civilized world.... (*The Teachers' Journal* 1936, p. 488)

School inspectors grappled with similar issues. Putland (1937, p. 42) commented on the 'teaching of civics in relation to recent international developments' and wondered how the 'rise to power of new nation states' and the 'application of science for war-like purposes' were affecting 'civic teaching in schools'. He concluded that 'every lesson should be a lesson in socialized living'. A school inspector from country NSW reflected that the post-primary curriculum:

[s]hould recognize that the child is a citizen in the making, a prospective worker, and an independent personality.... the objectives of such a course should be: 1) The development of ethical ideals 2) physical development 3) worthy home membership 4) preparation for vocational needs 5) appreciation of the responsibility of citizenship, and 6) capacity for using leisure hours worthily. (*The Sydney Morning Herald* 1932, p. 6)

Civics education is accorded a pivotal role in the curriculum, providing the basis for individual development and for building national strength of character. While the concerns were often mundane, personal and domestic in nature (managing leisure, preparing for work), this was accompanied by an insistence on seeing and understanding one's place in the wider world. Freedom of individual inquiry was linked to the achievement of freedom and democratic processes on a larger national and international scale.

The Australian Teacher magazine featured numerous articles throughout the 1930s on how to implement citizenship education and in which curriculum area, for example, 'History as training for citizenship' (Gooch 1930) or 'The history book and the citizen' (Oglivie 1937). In Victoria at least, history was indeed the subject area in which civics was most often taught during this period. The 1934 report on *The teaching of history and civics in Victorian secondary schools* by Alice Hoy provided an influential guide to teachers. Hoy, as a 'final Honours scholar in history' at Melbourne University, had previously co-authored an *Australasian text book of civics* with I.D. Marshall, Mistress of method, also at Melbourne University (Marshall and Hoy 1917). The textbook was re-issued several times throughout the 1920s and 1930s, and by 1937 it was sole-authored by Hoy, then lecturer in Method of History, and entitled *Civics in Australian schools* (Hoy 1937). Sections of the book were updated and new information added along the way, for example, in the aftermath of the Great War and the establishment of international agencies such as the League of Nations. The later edition was more focused on Australia's political systems and forms of government, whereas the earlier edition opened with a view to the beginnings of civilisation and discussion of the British parliament. The challenge of working out Australia's status in the wider world, particularly affiliations to empire in a changing political environment, was evident in these textbooks. By 1937, explanations of Australia's place in the world centred not only on her relation to Britain but also on her relations to a wider international community, although the question of empire continued to be addressed in a dedicated chapter. The final chapters of the 1937 edition focused on Australia and the world, the role of international law and international agencies, yet returned to the responsibility of Australia's citizens to uphold the values of obedience to the law and loyalty to the 'British race' (Hoy 1937, p. 132): in a multi-racial empire, however, only some could claim belonging to the British race.

Hoy's report on *The teaching of history and civics in Victorian secondary schools* (1934) lamented the state of civics teaching, holding teachers responsible for treating it as an examinable subject rather than a subject with a close relation to actual life (p. 41). A survey of teachers' views on the efficacy and content of civics found that many turned to examination results as an indicator of success, while others reported that the results of civics teaching could be seen in '"a ready recognition that there are many sides to every question and each has a right to be heard", a willingness to suggest and act, and a general alertness' (Hoy 1934, pp. 48–49). Hoy praised the cultivation of an attitude of 'world-mindedness' among pupils, and noted the positive impact of the League of Nations Schools' Day, first held in Melbourne in August 1932, in fostering such an outlook (p. 48). The distinctive phrase 'world-mindedness' was also employed by a contributor to *The journal of inspectors of schools of Australia,* who observed that revised courses in Victorian schools were giving history, geography and civics greater prominence (Osborne 1937, p. 16) and were aiming towards the ideals of 'tolerance and world mindedness' (p. 17).

We see here a clear expression of the idea of civics education as fostering cosmopolitan aspirations, alongside a mild tension arising from balancing knowledge of national systems and identifications with an orientation to looking beyond national shores and beyond the endorsement of single – individual or national – points of view. Internationalism and reasoned judgement were coupled, and civics was charged with realising these goals above and beyond the enhancement of specific content knowledge or the facts of the electoral system.

For Hoy, the real test of any curriculum reform or teaching of civics was the longer term question of 'Do pupils develop into good citizens?' Her response was measured:

> Only time will tell. But they are on the right road if they leave school with a good general knowledge of our political institutions, an easily roused interest in public affairs, a ready recognition of the fact that since there are two sides to every question it is folly to champion one side without trying to get to the point of view and

arguments of the other side; if they are becoming accustomed to listening patiently to views they may not agree with, since each side has an equal right to be heard; if they grasp the central fact which civics should teach, that every privilege implies a corresponding responsibility that must on no account be disregarded or lost through misuse. (Hoy 1934, p. 49)

Throughout this report – and evident too in the commentary of contemporary educators – there is a repeated emphasis on the need for students to recognise and respect different points of view. These were essential attributes not only of a good student but also for building a properly democratic society and future. Looking to the ideas of the British NEF as a leading authority on progressivism, the editorial of a 1939 issue of the Victorian *The Teachers' Journal* endorsed the NEF's view that: 'We must foster the habit of independent thought and expression of opinion and seek to establish the method of discussion and persuasion rather than compulsion' (p. 203).

Such strategies, it was proposed, would help make 'democracy part of the mental life of our children'. Yet this very pedagogical approach also raised fears about the threat of indoctrination and the vulnerability of young people to propaganda. 'Are we not therefore open to the charge of seeking to determine the attitude of our pupils towards life?' queried the editorial. 'We must admit this, but is it not the work of a teacher in a democracy?' Democratic-minded advocates of civics education had to straddle the tension between freedom of expression and guidance towards preferred political views. This was best achieved, it was argued, by instilling an attitude of fearless questioning, even of the status quo: 'We must, however, keep in mind that the outlook we are trying to foster includes the right of question and rejection, even of fundamentals'.

Quoting directly from the NEF's UK magazine, *New Era,* the editorial of the Victorian *Teachers' Journal* advocated that:

1. We must press for an education system which shall be fully democratic.
2. We must conduct our educational institutions in such a manner that the democratic ideal is experienced as a direct way of living.
3. We must make co-operation a day-by-day reality, giving each individual a feeling of responsibility for the whole and a share in determining the common life of himself and his fellows.
4. We must foster the habit of independent thought and expression of opinion.
5. We must accept as a matter of course respect for the individual conscience.
(*The Teachers' Journal* 1939, pp. 203–204)

Such exhortations align the aims of education for democracy and democratic forms of schooling with pedagogies that promote practices of perspective-taking and self-critical habits of mind. The preferred student had the capacity to determine their own points of view, to make rational judgements, to understand alternative positions and to do so with a self-conscious world-mindedness. The good student embodied a cosmopolitan and also relativist ideal. Yet this ideal had an underside. Popkewitz (2008) argues that cosmopolitanism itself is a dividing practice, a 'system of reason' that governs people and regulates processes of social inclusion and exclusion. Cosmopolitanism represents, he suggests, more than the cultivation of a worldly outlook or the appreciation of difference, and something other than the expression of a common humanity amidst national or cultural diversity (Popkewitz 2008, pp. 1–4). Rather, it is a 'particular mode of organizing difference' which 'entails comparative installations that differentiate and divide those who are enlightened and civilized from those who do not have those qualities – the backward, the savage, and the barbarian of the 19th century and the at-risk and delinquent child of the present' (2008, p. 4). Cosmopolitanism has, Popkewitz argues, a 'double gesture': 'Pedagogical narratives and images of cosmopolitanism simultaneously embody the two gestures of hope and fear' (Popkewitz 2008, pp. 1–4). A double gesture of 'hope and fear' animated discourses on the education and educability of adolescents in Australia during the 1930s. The overt and repeated hopefulness for the future (Australian) citizen simultaneously concealed and discursively constructed its other, the young (Aboriginal) person defined by an inability to achieve the uplifting dispositions of world-mindedness and clear-mindedness.

This division is brought to the fore in juxtaposing the educational problems debated at the two international conferences summarised above. At one level, the conferences appeared to represent different endeavours – education of the native and education for complete living. Yet I am suggesting it is precisely this apparent difference that makes a revealing comparison: both tackled difficult questions about the education and educability of the adolescent in relation to changing educational and political environments, yet with no apparent reference to the concerns of the other. This is especially remarkable as the conferences were held in consecutive years and were supported by similar international networks and funding. They represented two realms of expert knowledge, operating separately yet addressing related problems. This marked divisions between the worldly, critical citizen of progressive education and the anthropologically defined Indigenous adolescent subject, whose educability was compromised by ties to tradition and local community. Against the universal claims of brotherly love and democracy for all, the elevation of world-mindedness by progressive educators worked to make local affiliations problematic and the antithesis to the educated and educable citizen subject.

Education for Complete Living, 1937

The 1937 NEF conference *Education for Complete Living: The Challenge of Today* was part of a series of conferences convened by the UK-based NEF. The NEF was founded in 1921 under the leadership of Mrs Beatrice Ensor, a former inspector of secondary schools in Britain, and a theosophist whose approach to education and progressivism had also been influenced by the ideas of Maria Montessori (Brehony 2004, Middleton 2012). Ensor cultivated extensive international networks and promoted the ideas of the NEF through various publications, including its magazine *New Era in Education*, and a host of meetings and lectures. The NEF sponsored national and local branches, and convened educational conferences, initially in Europe and then further afield to the former colonies and dominions. The NEF described itself as a 'rallying point for people of all countries who felt that a radical reform of education, based on a proper understanding of childhood and of the unity in diversity of mankind, was essential if ever world peace was to be assured' (New Education Fellowship 1946). Its philosophy and approach were motivated by egalitarian and democratic principles and an optimistic view of the emancipatory promise of education to promote 'international friendship and co-operation' (Abbiss 1998).

A substantial body of research exists on the impact of the NEF, its version of progressive education and the role of its international conferences in aiding the circulation of their ideas and ideals within and beyond Europe (Jenkins 2000, Brehony 2004, Fuchs 2004, Godfrey 2004, Campbell and Sherington 2006). This scholarship forms part of the backdrop to the discussion here. With regard to citizenship education, the NEF advocated views and principles that met ready support among Australian educators involved in civics teaching and curriculum, most notably in the emphasis on the transformative potential of clear thinking and the capacity to think beyond oneself – individually and nationally. These topics were extensively debated at the 1937 conference.

As with previous NEF conferences, the Australian conference brought together a mix of international experts to debate the status and future of schooling and progressive educational reform. The conference was organised in Australia through the ACER, enthusiastically supported by its director, Kenneth Cunningham, who had been impressed by the 1934 NEF conference he had attended in South Africa and proposed that a similar event be held in Australia. The conference enacted the NEF principles of promoting community exchange and dialogue, and was held over a period of six to seven weeks, travelling through the capital cities of Australia, engaging with educators, teachers and the interested general public in well-attended meetings. The 1937 conference started in Brisbane on 4 August 1937, moving through the capital cities of Sydney, Canberra, Melbourne, Hobart, and Adelaide and ending in Perth on 18 September 1937 (Connell 1980, p. 107). Guest speakers included a number of US experts, many affiliated with Teachers College, Columbia, with New Education advocates from Switzerland, Austria, South Africa, Japan, New Zealand, Scotland, England, Canada, Denmark and Finland.[2]

It was a very successful event with high rates of attendance – attracting a total of 8718 participants across the seven sessions[3] – and received extensive press coverage (Connell 1980, pp. 103–116, Godfrey 2004). In reflecting on its impact, Cunningham considered the conference to have been of 'the greatest interest and importance to a country like Australia which is handicapped by its isolation' (Cunningham 1937), later observing that: 'During the five months that have elapsed since the termination of the conference there has been a steady accumulation of evidence that it is likely to have a definite effect on the course of Australian education' (Cunningham 1938b). The conference covered a wide range of topics from school curriculum to world affairs, examinations, teacher training, administration, and psychology and the schoolchild.[4] Many papers directly addressed the teaching of civics and citizenship education, including presentations on 'Education and world affairs', 'Nationalism and internationalism in education', 'Adapting education to modern needs', 'Education and social problems' and 'The school curriculum, with special attention to the subjects of social studies, history, mathematics, geography and the curriculum in the child-centred classroom' (Cunningham 1938a).

The conference combined expression of the lofty progressive ideals and internationalist principles of the NEF alongside more sober assessments of perceived problems and challenges with education in Australia, such as those seen by US delegates to arise from its centralised system of administration (Kandel 1938). While a good many of the papers bore the influence of progressivism and child-centred learning, a smaller number reflected the growing influence of mental testing and psychologically based classification of students (Glotzer 2009), with presentations on individual and group differences, and special learning and educational needs. In relation to the citizenship-building aims of education, however, three themes stand out, all signalling the promise of a new era: the need for curriculum reform and practical education in the civics area, the value of cultivating a world-minded outlook, and pedagogies to foster independence of mind.

Laurin Zilliacus (1938, p. 3), a headmaster from Finland and chairman of the NEF, saw the challenges confronting the world as representing 'the race between education and catastrophe' and pursuing robust democracy as the way to avoid social and political disaster: 'School for democracy', he exhorted, must 'give the *knowledge* required by the good citizen' (p. 10), and this must be more than old-fashioned, backward-looking content, not simply '1066 and all that'. Schools needed to teach current affairs abreast of social developments: 'History should be brought up to date. More ambitiously, and also more specifically, it means that matter should be included that is too new and too controversial to be found in textbooks' (p. 10). Schools should also provide '*practical training* in citizenship', allowing students to participate in self-government, caring for their surroundings, and assisting in 'the general maintenance of law and order' (p. 11). The most important way schools could serve democracy, he saw, was for them to 'foster the development of the *will to citizenship*: it should not only *charge* the mind, it should *touch* the mind – and the heart – of the growing generation. This task is partly intellectual, and partly emotional' (p. 11, italics in original):

> The intellectual task is to clarify the concept of democracy, to stimulate thought and discussion about its meaning, to trace its roots in love of freedom and truth and justice and a sense of oneness with our fellows, to develop the habit of confronting theory with practice and different components of our theory with each other so that they may modify each other and be brought into harmony. The emotional task is essentially to arouse a social conscience. (p. 12)

This led Zilliacus to reflect on the risk of indoctrination and the challenge of managing the views that teachers may pass on to pupils. While the ethical teacher should not pass on 'specific programmes adopted by competing political groups', he should 'do all he can to win devotion to the ideals on which democracy rests: love of truth, freedom and justice, and sense of the worth of the individual human life and respect for the individual conscience, and equally a sense of social responsibility' (p. 12). Such worries about the extent of the teacher's guiding role resonate with concerns also expressed by Australian educators (noted above); in both cases, the antidote to the risk of indoctrination was the cultivation in students of reasoned judgement, the capacity to understand the perspectives of others while at the same time exercising autonomy and freedom of thought. The burden for ethical judgement thus fell to teachers and their adoption of pedagogies that aided students' critical and reflexive thinking.

Capturing the concern with a broad understanding of citizenship education as part of the development of the 'whole self' and as based in practical experience, Boyd (1938) (Head of the Department of Education, Glasgow University) reflected:

> Citizenship is not merely or mainly a matter of voting or holding political office. The good citizen is the good member of society in all its aspects: good neighbour, good family man, good politician. ... [w]e must clear our minds of the idea that we can make good citizens by imparting information about social duties or by moral injunctions. Good citizenship is a right way of life, which can be bettered by an intelligent understanding of the facts of civic behaviour but depends on participation in community experience. (1938, p. 191)

Such direct participation helped foster 'education for social intelligence', which F.W. Hart (Professor of Education, University of California) regarded as essential for navigating the complexities and dangers of modern life and for properly recognising 'the inter-dependence of nations' (1938, pp. 16–18). He reflected:

> If and when social intelligence becomes the core and meat of the curriculum of our educational programme for youths and adults throughout the world, a League of Nations – a World Federation – will be formed, and international understanding will become a reality. (p. 17)

Bringing together internationalism and child-centred developmentalism, Bovet (1938) (Professor of Pedagogy at the University of Geneva and director of the

J.J. Rousseau Institute for Educational Sciences) constructed the shift from national to international concerns as a maturational process, with nationalism a less mature expression of affiliations and internationalism an expression of evolved humanism. Advancing the intrinsic merit of child-centred principles, Bovet (1938, p. 19) argued that it was still possible to have lessons which began with the child's interests, their local world, and cultivate an outlook onto the world beyond: 'There is no contradiction between this egocentric view of things and a continually widening outlook on the world: the child may remain in the centre, and the circle around this centre grows wider and wider' (p. 19). Indeed for Bovet, the pedagogical act of leading towards an 'ever-widening outlook' aids the developmental progress of the child from 'self-centred, to a truly human point of view' (p. 20). He advocated an 'all-embracing "we-consciousness"' (p. 20), looking to the 'full-realization of world-citizenship, of world-brotherhood' 'by way of reason' and taking as an example the disciples of Socrates, 'who first saw themselves as Cosmopolitans' (p. 22). Bovet's arguments regarding the developmental shift from the ego-centric and local world of the child to a 'truly human' and more worldly view provide a revealing point of contrast with the construction of localism and maturity in debates about the educability of Aboriginal students.

Education in Pacific Countries, 1936

A year before the 1937 Australian Fellowship of Education conference, an international seminar-conference on *Education in Pacific Countries* was held at the University of Hawaii in Honolulu, co-sponsored by that University and Yale (through its Department of Race Relations). A significant conference at the time, reports published from it offer vivid insights into the colliding discourses of internationalism and colonialism in education and reveal competing understandings of cultural differentiation and the educability of young people – topics of much current interest in educational research. Yet, surprisingly, this event appears somewhat neglected in contemporary scholarship, overshadowed in the historiography of interwar education and internationalism by research on activities of the League of Nations or the NEF and its well-known congresses. While it is not possible here to develop an in-depth analysis of the educational ideas debated at the conference, I make an initial attempt at contrasting the inclusive and internationalist ideals of progressivism with the agendas for Aboriginal education. In doing so, I attempt to show something of cosmopolitanism's 'double gesture' (Popkewitz 2008) of hope and fear. I question what a post-colonial reading of progressive aspirations might reveal, speculating that the pervasive influence of progressivism also served to undermine possibilities for the education of Aboriginal youth, who were implicitly excluded from and constituted as other to the normatively worldly and independent-minded adolescent.

In 1938, a report on the conference (written by the conference organiser, Felix Keesing) was published, although press coverage and reports from delegates had previously circulated in Australia. The conference report was, as the subtitle indicates, Keesing's interpretation of discussions at the event. It drew on papers presented with generous excerpts and recounted differences of opinions: unlike the Fellowship of Education proceedings, it is not a compilation of papers but a synthesis of discussions. Approximately 65 participants were in attendance, coming from 'Australia and its tropical dependencies, Papua and New Guinea', China, French Indo-China, Great Britain and 'certain of its Pacific colonies, British Malaya, Hong Kong and Fiji, and the Gilbert and Ellice islands', India, Japan, Latin America, the Netherlands East Indies, 'New Zealand and its mandated territory, Western Samoa', South Africa, the mainland United States, 'including spokesmen for the Negro and American Indian', the Philippines and American Samoa, and Hawaii (Keesing 1938, pp. 1–2). Australia was represented by four delegates, not one an educationalist, although representatives from other countries included school inspectors, directors of education, elementary school principals and teachers, missionaries and a 'colonial administrator' (Keesing 1938, p. 2). The Australian representatives were Professor A.P. Elkin, an anthropologist from the University of Sydney, Mr F.E. Williams, government anthropologist of Papua, Mr William Groves, social anthropologist, Australian National Research Council and Mr Norman Tindale, Ethnologist, Adelaide Museum (*The Canberra Times* 1936, p. 4). A.P. Elkin was a vocal contributor to the conference and wrote several reports and articles en route to the conference and on his return (Elkin 1936, 1936/37). In January 1937, *The Argus* reported that Elkin believed the conference would be regarded as a 'landmark in the education of native peoples', summarising that the conference considered problems of 'national culture and educational policies for native races and the aims and philosophy of such education' (*The Argus* 1937, p. 16).

Topics addressed over the course of the conference included the following: comparative reflections on national education systems and approaches to the education of the native; education and nationalism; 'assimilation versus indigenous development in education'; 'persons of racially mixed descent and their educational problems'; 'the significance of racial differences, particularly as applying to education; the comparative educability of peoples' (Keesing 1938, p. 5). An overall aim of the conference was to identify common problems, programmes and principles for the education of the native, yet at the heart of the conference agenda was a concern with differentiation and elaboration of cultural and educational hierarchies. Central problems addressed throughout the conference were: 'Do racial groups differ in their educability?' and 'Are there peoples who must be educated in special ways because of their racial limitations, or who are even not worth trying to educate at all'? (p. 46). Responses to these questions varied according to the perceived potential of different racial groups, with some groups considered more or less educable than others. The 'Australian Aborigine', Keesing reported, was judged to be a 'very specialized type of humanity ... [with] no carefully considered plan of education worked out to meet their needs' (Keesing 1938, p. 22). Summarising the views of Australian delegates, Keesing continued:

> In the main, the aim has been "protection" rather than education. The "protector of aborigines" and the policeman are the main agents of government contact, and schooling so far as it exists has been left almost entirely to mission bodies.

Concluding, Keesing (1938, p. 22) wondered whether this:

> strangely deviant people really can respond to an educational program shaped to their actual needs and conditions, or indeed whether any adequate system can be worked out in relation to their isolated, scattered, and often still nomadic remnants, has yet to be determined.

Although it was generally accepted among delegates that native peoples could 'adopt things western [and] that cultural elements can spread entirely independently of race', some felt that a 'few extremely deviant peoples, notably the Australian Aborigine, the pygmy Negrito and the Ainu, might be quite unable to adapt themselves to modernity or produce individuals who could climb far up the ladder of modern scholarship' (Keesing 1938, pp. 50–51). This hierarchy of racial capacity and developmentalism was contested at the time, with intense debates among delegates, particularly regarding the relative force of cultural environment and practices against alleged inherent capacity. The Australian anthropologist, A.P. Elkin, for example, disagreed with the assessment of the limited educability of Aboriginal people, warning fellow participants not to 'undervalue their intelligence because of their existence of certain aboriginal cultural traits which seem to us as superstitious or primitive' (reported in Keesing 1938, p. 51). In his 1936 paper written in advance and presented at the conference, Elkin advanced a more culturally relativist view, observing that 'the educator's basic assumption' is that:

> all races are educable even to the higher grades, and until all social and economic handicaps have been removed, no modification of that assumption, based on psychological or biological grounds, is possible; races are different because their cultures and histories differ. (Elkin 1936, p. 153)

Elkin insisted that conference members acknowledged the complex knowledge systems into which Aboriginal people were inducted 'through personal instruction, by ritual and symbol and explanation' (Elkin in Keesing 1938, p. 51):

> Intelligence tests apart, the social anthropologist cannot but regard many of his native informants as intelligent educated men and women. Their ability to discuss the intricacies of the kinship system, the local and totemic organization and the bearing of these on marriage and behaviour, and on one another is one

evidence of this; the way in which they think out ways of convincing the doubting investigator of the validity of their beliefs and the remarkable and logically correct methods by which they adjust the kinship section, moiety and other variable forms of social order of different tribes to one another: these facts are sufficient evidence of the educability of the Aborigines to take their place in a complex cultural system. (Elkin in Keesing 1938, pp. 50–51)

Yet Elkin's own position was somewhat contradictory, and his views written after the conference reflected a more hierarchical model of racial capacity, identifying definite developmental limits to the educability of Aboriginal children.

The growing influence of psychological classifications and intelligence testing was also apparent in conference deliberations, adding fuel to 'nature' versus 'culture' debates, with worried questions about whether tests measure 'innate ability' or 'attainment within a given cultural setting' (Keesing 1938, p. 55). This reflected a clash of ideas – also evident in the Fellowship of Education conference proceedings – over the status and authority of 'scientific testing', belief in the equality of opportunity and a child-centred educational doctrine. The dominant message was a hybrid of these educational and ethical positions. As one delegate declared, 'We are going to give equality of opportunity to all peoples at least until their inequality has been factually and scientifically demonstrated' (reported in Keesing 1938, p. 57).

I want to identify two significant points of difference between the representation of the educability of Aboriginal children and the educability of the implicitly white student hailed in the exhortations of New Education and citizenship education: a contrast between independent and passive learning that also maps onto a distinction between internationalism and localism; and a contrast between adolescence as a blossoming of identity leading to autonomy and adolescence as a closing down of opportunities for education and freedom. A clear pedagogical point of division between Aboriginal and white children was the method of rote learning (an anathema for progressives). Elkin (1936/37) reported that Aboriginal children, at least until the age of puberty, had been able to do well in mission schools, sometimes outperforming white pupils. But this was, he explained, due to the predominance of rote learning, which suited the mental habits of the Aborigine for whom rote learning is important in their daily life. Similarly, Aboriginal children showed great skill in mastery of manual arts:

> but they lag behind in arithmetic, and show but little power of expressing their thoughts in writing: indeed in most cases... ability to express thoughts in words seems lacking. The tendency of the native pupils is to try to learn everything in parrot fashion and not to get an intelligent grip of the lesson. (Elkin 1936/37, p. 489)

The relatively low achievements and mental age of Aboriginal children were attributed to 'the absence of ambition, incentive and home encouragement' (Elkin 1936/37, p. 490).

In such commentary, the Aboriginal child is positioned as the antithesis to the opinion-forming, independent-minded pupil hailed by New Education. Any achievement in education is linked to mastery of practical skills and passive learning, in contrast to the reflexive learning associated with the child of progressivism. Further, the capacity for educability was seen to have developmental limits. Whatever one's views on the mental capacity and educability of Aboriginal children, Elkin argued, and 'whatever progress is made before puberty, it stops then' (p. 491). At puberty, the pull of family and ritual life is so strong that it counters the call of education: 'the fascination with hunting, camping, marriage and the secret life, and their heart will be in those outside interests'. In looking to cultural explanations for this turning away from education, Elkin (1936/37, p. 492) suggests that adolescents, 'as well as their parents know that there is for them really no independent future commensurate with the goal towards which our educational system leads'.

Cultural explanations, however, were readily countered by biological developmentalism. The onset of puberty provided another reason for stunted development and a turning away from education and that is, Elkin argued, the 'comparatively early development of, or absorption in, the sex impulses' (Elkin 1936/37). According to Elkin, it was the co-incidence of this with the experience of race prejudice and the knowledge that 'they are not wanted in white social and economic life' that confirmed Aboriginal children's retreat from education and a 'mental falling off'; this was exacerbated by being 'thrown in upon themselves in an ever-dulling environment'. Entry to adolescence and the onset of puberty were represented in the language of decline and loss: a loss of 'practically all the refinements they had acquired, and [they] find happiness in what is to us the dirty, ill-fed and uncertain life of the moving camp' (Elkin 1936/37, p. 493).

The second contrast then, with the imagined adolescent represented in the cosmopolitan aspirations for citizenship education and given expression in the proceedings of the Fellowship of Education, is that the implied white pupil enters adolescence as an opening up, as a blossoming of possibilities, of the taking up of higher-order thinking and judgement. Whereas for the Aboriginal pupil, adolescence is marked by decline, by being less open to education, less educable in part because they are more embedded in and constrained by their familial and local world. Adolescence was a time when bodily and hormonal drives and kin relations and responsibilities overtook Aboriginal children, and kept them at an arrested stage of development. Adolescence for white children was a time of freedom, aspiring to greater autonomy, the embrace of rationality and independence of mind. Conversely, Aboriginal children were constrained, their once detectable natural intelligence subordinated by local networks and biological drives. Progressivism's call for world-mindedness and clear-mindedness produced the adolescent subject entwined in family and local relations as problematic, as the other to a cosmopolitan ideal. Instead of questions about education for citizenship and worldliness, the question of education for Aboriginal adolescents became framed as a problem of educability and identity.

Conclusion

In my opening remarks, I noted debates among Australian schoolteachers regarding whether citizenship education should be cosmopolitan or nationalist in orientation. While cosmopolitanism was thus a zone of contestation it was, nevertheless, an influential set of beliefs and interrogations informing an array of educational practices and pedagogical interventions. It also promised a new type of student-citizen, the worldly subjects of modernity, able to position themselves reflexively, appreciate the relativity of perspective and the inter-dependence of nations. In the background to debates about the nationally or internationally minded student – yet not usually admitted into the same discussions – were the education and identity of Aboriginal students, whose affiliations and orientations were constructed as not international and only potentially or incipiently national but as deeply and problematically local. I have illustrated some of the dividing practices of citizenship education and looked to how cosmopolitanism's double gesture of hope and fear constituted the desired student and its other, in this case Indigenous students who could not escape from the burdens of familial and local affiliations.

The idealised cosmopolitan student not only was a free and critical thinker, but also wore their national identity lightly. The Aboriginal student, in contrast, bore a heavier burden of identity, with their kinship and family networks drawing them inwards at the very time – adolescence – that non-Aboriginal students were seen to flourish and embrace autonomy. Pierre Bovet, at the Fellowship of Education conference, saw no inconsistency in moving the child from a local to a worldly outlook and, indeed, saw this as one of the features of child-centred progressivism. Yet in debates about the educability of young Aboriginal people, the local represented not the possibility of movement forward, but the threat of backward-looking confinement.

Finally, I have attempted to raise questions about the racialising and colonising dimensions of progressive education, to consider the ways in which this hopeful and even utopian educational movement made some student-citizens problematic, as beyond or irrelevant to the cosmopolitan ideal, even as that ideal could be seen to exacerbate their very exclusions. In this preliminary way, I hope to have opened up some possibilities for more fully developing a post-colonial account of progressive education's democratic and inclusive promise.

Acknowledgements

This article draws from a larger historical study of Australian adolescence and citizenship education, 1930s–1970s: *Educating the Australian adolescent: an historical study of curriculum, student counselling and citizenship, 1930s–1970s*, Australian Research Council Discovery Grant 2009–2012. The principal researchers are Julie McLeod and Katie Wright with research fellows Sari Braithwaite, Sophie Rudolph and Amy McKernan. Project website: http://www.edfac.unimelb.edu.au/eaa. The author acknowledges with thanks the contributions of all team members, and also thanks Katie Wright for her helpful suggestions in the development of this paper.

Notes

1. For a biographical note on Keesing, see the entry for his papers at the archives of the University of Hawai'i at Manoa: http://libweb.hawaii.edu/libdept/archives/univarch/faculty/indiv/keesing.htm
2. For further discussion on the organisation and impact of this and related conferences and the role of the Carnegie Corporation of New York in supporting these transnational networks, see Lawn (2004), White (1997) and Glotzer (2009).
3. Cunningham (1938b); attendance numbers were: Brisbane 1343, Sydney 1847, Melbourne 2302, Hobart 677, Adelaide 1175, Perth 1374.
4. The conference proceedings are organised according to the following sections: Education and world affairs; The new outlook in education; Education and social problems; Education and rural life; Educational administration, research and teacher training; Examinations; The school curriculum; Special aspects of education; Adolescent and adult education; The university; and The psychological and mental life of the school child. See also Campbell and Sherington (2006) for a synopsis of conference themes.

References

Abbiss, J., 1998. The 'New Education Fellowship' in New Zealand: its activity and influence in the 1930s and 1940s. *New Zealand journal of educational studies*, 33 (1), 81–93.

Bovet, P., 1938. Nationalism and internationalism in education. *In:* K.S. Cunningham, ed. *Education for complete living: the challenge of to-day, the proceedings of the New Education Fellowship conference*, 1 August–20 September 1937, Australia. Melbourne: Australian Council for Educational Research, 19–23.

Boyd, W., 1938. Education and citizenship. *In:* K.S. Cunningham, ed. *Education for complete living: the challenge of to-day, the proceedings of the New Education Fellowship conference*, 1 August–20 September 1937, Australia. Melbourne: Australian Council for Educational Research, 191–192.

Brehony, K., 2004. A new education for a new era: the contribution of the conferences of the New Education Fellowship to the disciplinary field of education 1921–1938. *Paedagogica historica*, 40 (5), 733–755.

Campbell, C. and Sherington, G., 2006. A genealogy of an Australian system of comprehensive high schools: the contribution of educational progressivism to the one best form of universal secondary education 1900–1940. *Paedagogica historica*, 42 (1–2), 191–210.

Connell, W.F., 1980. *The Australian council for educational research 1930–80*. Melbourne: Australian Council for Educational Research.

Cunningham, K.S., 1937. *Monthly news and notes*. No. 43 of the Australian Council for Educational Research, Archives of the WEF, Institute of Education, University of London, WEF/A/11/49, Australian Council for Educational Research, 1937–1947 [KS Cunningham].

Cunningham, K.S., ed., 1938a. *Education for complete living: the challenge of to-day, the proceedings of the New Education Fellowship conference*, 1 August–20 September 1937, Australia. Melbourne: Australian Council for Educational Research.

Cunningham, K.S., 1938b. *Monthly news and notes*. No. 44 [Feb] of the Australian Council for Educational Research, Archives of the WEF, Institute of Education, University of London, WEF/A/11/49, Australian Council for Educational Research, 1937–1947 [KS Cunningham].

Elkin, A.P., 1936. Education of native races in Pacific countries: report of a conference. *Oceania*, vii (2), 145–168.

Elkin, A.P., 1936/37. Native education, with special reference to the Australian Aborigines. *Oceania*, vii (2), 459–501.

Foucault, M., 1988. Technologies of the self. *In*: L.H. Martin, H. Gutman, and P.H. Hutton, eds. *Technologies of the self: a seminar with Michel Foucault*. London: Tavistock Publications, 16–49.

Fuchs, E., 2004. Educational sciences, morality and politics: international educational congresses in the early twentieth century. *Paedagogica historica*, 40 (6), 257–284.

Fuchs, E., 2007. The creation of new international networks in education. The League of Nations and educational organizations in the 1920s. *Paedagogica historica*, 43 (2), 199–209.

Glotzer, R., 2009. A long shadow: Frederick P. Keppel, the Carnegie corporation and the dominions and colonies fund area experts. *History of education*, 38 (5), 621–648.

Godfrey, J., 2004. 'Perhaps the most important, and certainly the most exciting event in the whole history of education in Australia': the 1937 New Education Fellowship conference and New South Wales examination reform. *History of education review*, 33 (2), 45–58.

Gooch, G.P., 1930. History as training for citizenship. *The Australian teacher*, 8 (2), 30–34.

Hart, F.W., 1938. Education for international understanding. *In:* K.S. Cunningham, ed. *Education for complete living: the challenge of to-day, the proceedings of the New Education Fellowship conference*, 1 August–20 September 1937, Australia. Melbourne: Australian Council for Educational Research, 14–18.

Hogben, E.B., 1937. The useful citizen. *The Teacher's Journal: A Practical aid for teachers to the Curriculum and Requirements of the Education Department of Victoria*, April, p. 138.

Hoy, A., ed., 1934. *Report on the teaching of history and civics in Victorian secondary schools*, by the History Sub-Committee of the Victorian Institute for Educational

Research. Melbourne: Melbourne University Press in association with Oxford University Press.

Hoy, A., 1937. *Civics for Australian schools*. Melbourne: Lothian Publishing.

Isin, E., 2002. *Being political: genealogies of citizenship*. Minneapolis, MN: University of Minnesota Press.

Jenkins, C., 2000. New education and its emancipatory interests (1920–1950). *History of education*, 29 (2), 139–151.

Kandel, I.L., 1938. Impressions of Australian education. *In:* K.S. Cunningham, ed. *Education for complete living: the challenge of to-day, the proceedings of the New Education Fellowship conference*, 1 August–20 September 1937, Australia. Melbourne: Australian Council for Educational Research, 649–660.

Keesing, F., 1938. *Education in Pacific countries: interpreting a seminar-conference of educators and social scientists conducted by the University of Hawaii and Yale University, Honolulu, Hawaii, 1936*. London: Oxford University Press.

Lawn, M., 2004. The institute as network: the Scottish Council for Research in Education as a local and international phenomenon in the 1930s. *Paedagogica historica*, 40 (5–6), 719–732.

Marshall, I.D. and Hoy, A., 1917. *Australasian text book of civics*. Melbourne: The Lothian Book Publishing Company.

Meredyth, D. and Thomas, J., 1999. A civics excursion: ends and means for old and new citizenship education. *History of education review*, 28 (2), 1–15.

Middleton, S., 2012. Clare Soper's hat: New Education Fellowship correspondence between Bloomsbury and New Zealand. *History of Education*. Available from: http://www.tandfonline.com/doi/abs/10.1080/0046760X.2012.678889 [Accessed 5 July 2012].

New Education Fellowship, 1946. *Education for international understanding held in Australia, 1946* [conference brochure]. Australia, Archives of the World Education Fellowship, Institute of Education Library, University of London, WEF/A/111/201.

Oglivie, V., 1937. The history book and the citizen. *The Australian teacher*, 15 (2), 23–27.

Osborne, G.A., 1937. The revised curriculum in Victorian elementary schools. *The journal of inspectors of schools of Australia*, 1 (1), 14–20.

Popkewitz, T.S., 2008. *Cosmopolitanism and the age of school reform*. New York: Palgrave.

Putland, F., 1937. The teaching of civics in relation to recent international developments. *The journal of inspectors of schools of Australia*, 1 (1), 42–46.

The Argus, 1937. Native education aborigines' view of Christianity. *The Argus*, 16 January, p. 16.

The Argus, 1938. Training children as citizens: divergent opinions of teachers: department asked to act. *The Argus*, 27 January, p. 2.

The Canberra Times, 1936. Conference at Honolulu: representatives of Australia. *The Canberra Times*, 3 June, p. 4.

The Sydney Morning Herald, 1932. The schools: post-primary courses. Country centres. *The Sydney Morning Herald*, 7 July, p. 6.

The Sydney Morning Herald, 1936. Educating a democracy. *The Sydney Morning Herald*, 24 January, p. 10.

The Teachers' Journal, 1936. Editorial: Education and democracy. *The Teachers' Journal: A Practical aid for teachers to the Curriculum and Requirements of the Education Department of Victoria*, October, p. 488.

The Teachers' Journal, 1939. Editorial: Education and democracy. *The Teachers' Journal*, 20 May, pp. 203–204.

White, M., 1997. Carnegie philanthropy in Australia in the nineteen thirties – a re-assessment. *History of education review*, 26 (1), 1–24.

Zilliacus, L., 1938. The race between education and catastrophe. *In*: K.S. Cunningham, ed. *Education for complete living: the challenge of to-day, the proceedings of the New Education Fellowship conference*, 1 August–20 September 1937, Australia. Melbourne: Australian Council for Educational Research, 3–13.

A new teacher for a new nation? Teacher education, 'English', and schooling in early twentieth-century Australia

Bill Green and Jo-Anne Reid

School of Teacher Education and the Research Institute for Professional Practice, Learning and Education (RIPPLE), Charles Sturt University, Bathurst, Australia

> The late nineteenth-century expansion of public schooling in Australia from an initial focus on the elementary phase to post-primary provision, and then to a more systematic secondary education over the early to mid-twentieth century, went hand in hand with the emergence of new populations of children and young people – a new constituency. In turn, these developments called into being a New Teacher, and a new system of teacher education, formed in accordance with what was widely understood as the New Education. Moreover, this was conceived as clearly in the service of nation-building. This paper traces aspects of the history of teacher education in Australia in the first half of the twentieth century, proposing that this is best understood with reference to the cultural and ideological significance of English teaching and the English language, nation and empire.

Introduction

In 1901, Professor William Mitchell of the University of Adelaide declared that South Australian teachers were the 'least educated in the English-speaking world' (Hyams 1979, p. 48). All around Australia at this time of the Federation, conservative elites were voicing statements of dissatisfaction with the quality of teachers, especially those in primary schools. Much of this criticism appears to have been directed, in particular, towards their poor standards of English expression and speech (Turner 1943), those aspects of the young Australian character most obviously dissimilar from that of Mother England. In this year, too, in New South Wales, for example, Professor Francis Anderson declared himself unable to join 'the conspiracy of adulation' with regard to the merits of the Public School system of education claimed by that state, 'or the conspiracy of silence with regard to its equally undoubted defects' (cited in Selleck 1968, p. vii). Public criticism of teachers was pervasive, with their defects of character, preparation and intellect widely noted in government, church and journalistic criticism (Turner 1943, Hyams 1976, Saunders 1976), which by its nature sought to establish the social credentials of the critics.

Saunders' (1976, p. 5) acerbic comment, that 'one of the paradoxes of education is that parents have been so prepared to hand over their children to the care of persons they openly despise', is resonant of this situation, and yet it remains disturbing, given our now extensive work in researching the history of English teaching, teacher education and public schooling in Australia from Federation to World War II. How is it that teachers, and public school teachers more generally, have been regarded so negatively for so long, when they have been equally centrally implicated in shaping Australia as a nation, from its very inception? What *investments* are at issue?

Grosvenor and Lawn (2001) have argued that teacher identity is usefully understood, historically, as thoroughly intertwined with national identity – indeed, in this case, teacher identity and the formation of teacher identity need to be thought of in relation to 'official nationalism' and the strategic (re)production of 'Englishness'. From this point of view, constructing the Teacher and forming the Nation are complementary and congruent practices in the Australian context (Green and Reid 2002). Here, we further explore the emergence and consolidation of a new system of teacher education and a new formulation of teacher identity in the first four decades of the twentieth century, and of 'Australia'. We argue that this new teacher was a strategic, planned invention – conceived, right from the outset, as an index of the Nation. Moreover, the new teacher was a crucial figure in nation-building (Green 2003). Pedagogic authority went hand in hand with the authority of the newly emergent nation-state, as a distinctive identity – one that needed for the nation's survival to be closely aligned to a sense of the 'Home' from which it came. As the Victorian educator Browne (1927) put it: 'An attractive but very responsible task is confronting the teaching profession in Australia. It is that of guiding this great British nation in the south through the critical years of its youth' (p. xxi).

Browne's latter phrase is especially telling, and drawing attention to it here is apposite: teachers and 'youth' are linked together both discursively and metaphorically. The early to mid-twentieth century has been described as a distinctive phase in the preparation of Australian teachers, in accordance with, on the one hand, the consolidation and further development of primary schooling (Spaull 1998) and, on the other, the formal extension of public provision to the secondary ('post-primary') level. Schooling now effectively reached from the very earliest years of primary schooling, through various versions of secondary education, to the university – for some, at least (Whitehead and Wilkinson 2008). Those young Australians who were selected by examination as worthy of 'superior' or 'higher' schooling beyond a primary education were already an academic élite, and thereby given the opportunity to lift themselves into a higher social class, alongside those whose parents could pay for secondary education and entry to the professions. Schooling therefore now firmly brought together a new population of children and young people ('adolescents'), within the governmental ambit of the state.

'English' figured heavily in Australian schooling during this period. This was not simply in English teaching and the English subjects, newly installed at the very heart of the school curriculum, but also in the strong emphasis on *the English language*, as the general medium of instruction and learning. 'Englishness', and the capacity to speak the Mother tongue 'well', was also the register of culture and class. English in Australia was a complex negotiation of 'Nation' and 'Empire', language and culture, literacy and identity (Green and Cormack 2008). Australian 'slang' was to be eradicated and, although it remained celebrated in the popular press and the growing corpus of Australian literature, these were not the stuff of English lessons. The importance of English literature in terms of both the subject of English and the subjectivity of the citizens of the new Australian nation is clear. School children were to be taught the great classic verses and to read the literature of their British homeland. As South Australian teachers were told in 1910:

> well-illustrated books on stirring deeds in history, or on geography and travel, will do much to awaken a new interest in these subjects. Such a library of books, judiciously selected, will be a most powerful influence for good throughout the school, enriching the pupils' minds and helping to develop their character. (*The Education Gazette* 1910)

Accordingly, every teacher needed indeed to become and *be* 'a teacher of English', at every level, something clearly observed in the teacher education curriculum of the time, both in the new Teachers' Colleges and beyond. In (re)telling that story here, we use historical data collected in two Australian states and their various Teachers' Colleges, as well as more generally.[1] Understanding our past considerably advances understanding our present, and enables us to look more strategically into our future(s). We begin with an overview of the birth of the nation and the prospect for education.

A new nation

In 1901, the federation of British colonies established in the Great South Land resulted in a new nation – Australia. This was a time of growth in industry and commerce and the forging of new constructions of nationhood, for example, through involvement in the Great War. The major concerns of the new Federal government were trade with other countries, and 'immigration' – the important task of keeping Australia 'white', as 'this great British nation in the south' (Browne 1927, p. xxi) would need to be. The Federal government had little to do with the nation's children at all, and as noted in an early national review, it took 'no part in Education, which is entirely under the control of the State governments' (Browne 1927, p. xviii).

The nature of the problem that education was to solve for the new nation – and an explanation of the degree to which Australians looked 'home' to England for support and definition of British identity – is encapsulated in the following extract from the same report, an early history of Australian education. Browne (1927, p. xviii) continued his advice to the government with a call to acknowledge the uniqueness of 'Australia's educational problem' in consequence of its location, 'only a few days' sail from overwhelming millions of coloured peoples'. How Australia's small white population, 'almost entirely of British stock', was to 'keep her continent white' would be a problem not only for the bustling coastal trading ports and cities, but also for the remote and rural outback where British knowledge of agriculture and social structure was proving so inappropriate for the lonely land and climate 'out back'.

Keeping the Asian neighbours on their own side of the fence was a task for the new Federation. Indeed, ever since the gold rushes of the 1850s, the threat of Asian immigration has been high on the national agenda, and continues up to the present day (Fabian and Loh 1980, Rizvi 1997, Jayasuriya et al. 2003). At that time in Australia's history, the curriculum of the 'English subjects' was one of the educational strategies to serve this end – playing a significant role in ensuring that Australian children were immersed in language and literature that promoted, among other things, colonialist perceptions about the 'savages' of the 'antipodes' being saved through the civilising mission of Christianity, and the inherent superiority of the white races.

At this time, too, educationalists in Britain were responding to what they saw as the negative effects of curriculum practices 'obsessed with the Three R's to the neglect if not always the exclusion of other subjects', taught by 'cramming to obtain results at the examination' (Selleck 1968, pp. vii–viii, Selleck 1982, pp. 5–6). Educational reform in Britain was seen by Australian educational leaders as a model for innovation. The New Education was characterised as 'dependent upon the spontaneous development of the child's creative powers and instincts, which can only be aroused through activity and experience, not through books and the reproduction of the thoughts and ideas of others' (Boyd and Rawson 1965, p. ix). A 'new Syllabus' for primary schooling was introduced in the early twentieth century in New South Wales, as elsewhere (Meadmore 2003a, 2003b). It included a number of radical reforms to the curriculum and pedagogy, such as the 'correlation of subjects', and a focus on student activity as the basis of school instruction.

Selleck (1968, p. 10) saw this as 'the introduction of the culture, which had been the possession of the few, to everyone'. The love of the country so necessary for the nation's protection was to be engendered in its youth by access to its cultural heritage – so that 'the love of field and coppice' would continue to 'run in the veins' of Australian children and young people. While, by the end of World War I, when she wrote 'My Country', Australians like Dorothea McKellar were already reacting to the effects of this curriculum, teachers continued to provide Australian youth with the literature and history of the British Empire, through classroom activity that was intended to engage them though imagination and play, recreation and affirmation. Boyd and Rawson (1965, p. ix), in an international account of the New Education, noted that these reforms required that the teacher should come into closer touch with the pupils' homes and surroundings; and that they would embody the belief that school should be a powerful agent in the intellectual, moral and social development of children. This in turn would require a very different kind of teacher, and a new form of teacher education accordingly.

A 1902 NSW Royal Commission into education had sent two leading local educationalists, George Knibbs and John Turner, overseas to enquire into existing methods of instruction for primary, secondary, technical and other forms of educational provision, and to recommend on implementation of improvements to the NSW educational system (Cole 1927, Cormack 2004). Their report showed that, far from grinding facts into children, the progressive trends in education overseas assumed that 'the supreme aim of education is the development of human character' (Cole 1927). Such changes in the aims of education would have great implications for teacher education, as we discuss in the next section. They demanded a New Teacher.

Peter Board, Director of Public Instruction for NSW at this time, noted:

> the change from the old standard of Proficiency ... made a great demand on [teachers'] energy and resources. ... [T]hose teachers who regard teaching as equivalent to 'making children learn' will be, and are, at a loss in carrying out what the Syllabus requires. (Cole 1927, p. 35)[2]

As Cole (1927, p. 35) noted, the new century was bringing many changes to schools and schooling:

> paper supplanted slate, free writing partly replaced copybooks, silent reading was introduced, nature was studied at first hand, mathematics became one subject, and Euclid gave way to practical and experimental geometry. The Syllabus gradually brought about a singular reform ... the child being placed at the centre, and the teacher guiding even more than instructing.

However, in reality, reform to the new nation's school system was neither as widespread nor as effective as had been hoped. Preparation of the new teacher necessary for the children of the new Australian nation, and its New Education syllabuses, became the answer to a problem that urgently needed to be solved – particularly for the primary school. Existing teachers were ill-prepared for the changes, and, at the start of the century, new teachers were trained by a period of pupil-teaching under the tutelage of those already in service, or existing teachers. The philosophy of education and its resulting curriculum might change, but as Cole (1927, p. 18) ominously observed, the figure of 'the pupil teacher lingered ...':

> ... it was said that the pupil teacher mind dominated the system from top to bottom. [...] the men in charge of the administration have been trained within the system and are apparently unable to go beyond it; their minds move in a closed circle.

Teacher education

As the New Education took hold of the consciousness of local intellectuals, old-fashioned pupil-teacher methods of teacher training were no longer seen as adequate to the task of reform. Teachers for the New Education needed to know more than the 'facts' of the traditional primary school syllabus, and they needed to move beyond a pedagogy characterised by the 'severity, emotional distance and military-style discipline' (Theobald 1990, p. 26) that was popularly caricatured by Dickens' Mr Gradgrind. Moreover, the teaching and learning of *English* would be central to this new teacher education that would assist in constructing a viable Australian nation: 'The whole course focused on English' (Meadmore 2003b, p. 6). Closely linked with this need in primary teacher education was the fact that, as each state government sought to offer a secular secondary schooling, teachers capable of teaching beyond the primary level were needed. The need for all teachers to be well schooled in English was thus heightened. In a report to the 1904 NSW Parliament, for instance, the Trade and Commerce Committee noted:

> Great emphasis should be laid on writing, spelling, composition and reading. [...] It is strongly recommended that every subject in the curriculum should be regarded as an opportunity for teaching English, there being reason to believe that pupils are inclined to regard writing, spelling and clear expression of secondary importance in subjects other than English, and that at present there is insufficient check on this tendency. (NSW Parliament 1904, p. 4)

But changes were slow in coming. By 1914, Alexander Mackie, brought from Scotland in 1905 as the first Principal of the new Teachers' Training College in Sydney, and subsequently the foundation Professor of Education at Sydney University, noted that 'schooling is apt to be unduly conservative, and we have as yet, I believe, only partially realised the kind of teacher needed for the task of schooling in a modern democratic state' (Mackie 1915, p. 3).[3] Soon after his arrival, Mackie linked education with wider social progress, and stated that 'the educational problem is one part of the social problem and cannot be separated from it'. He clearly coupled the success of education and social progress with the training of teachers:

> Further, it is being more and more fully realised that a successful educational system is impossible without a professionally trained body of teachers, and that the personality and high professional character of the teachers is an essential, indeed the essential factor. (Mackie 1907, p. 9)

Training this significant group of the new nation's young people (adolescents themselves when they commenced their teacher training courses, and often still not 'adult' when they commenced teaching) to fit this important national work would be a challenge indeed. What sort of teacher education could develop in these young people both 'the intellectual interests and character traits desirable in a teacher' *and* 'the necessary technical preparation for a complex and specialised social service' (McRae and Turner 1943, p. 1)? McRae and Turner, looking back here over the first 40 years of the 'new' teacher education established in NSW at the turn of the century, clearly highlight the 'continuous compromise' involved in this 'dual task' of teacher education.

At the turn of the century, when Mackie and leading educational administrators such as Alfred Williams in South Australia and Frank Tate in Victoria were commissioned to raise the quality of teacher education, their task was already Sisyphean. Despite the Public Instruction Act of 1880, itself designed to improve the quality of teachers, 'the foundations only of training had been laid':

> [T]he pupil teacher system was an inadequate substitute for a real preparation for the teaching profession. Moreover, as far as the small country schools were concerned, many untrained people, who had not even the advantage of having been pupil teachers, continued to be appointed with practically no preparation at all. Only a limited number of Pupil Teachers, those who did best at their fourth annual examination, to the number of about thirty men and thirty women, were given a year's training at the Colleges .... (Cole 1927, p. 63)

For Browne, the root of the problem lay in the unhelpful geography of the new nation-continent:

> The truth is that centralization is the best form of educational rule for a young country with a vast hinterland. It ensures that the children of the rural pioneer receive as good an education as the children of the banker or artisan in the city, and Australia is proud of the efficiency of her small country schools ... [...] With so small a population dispersed over such an immense area, can her States develop and maintain effective systems of education? She has six magnificent cities, but the real educational problem lies with the small school, perhaps of only ten or twelve children, that is situated right out on the frontiers of agricultural development .... (Browne 1927, pp. xvii and xviii)

This was the 'Rural Problem' in education, which had dogged the new nation from well before its formal inception. For instance, a 'Pastoral and Agricultural' Sub-Committee of the NSW Legislative Council and Assembly, reporting to an inquiry into educational issues in 1904, raised 'an important question in regard to the country teacher'. This related to what was already a well-established perception that:

> frequent changes, with the hope of ultimate appointment to a city school, tend to lessen the teacher's interest in the education of the rural child. Indeed, it was suggested that the teacher's own unrest might tend to lessen the rural-mindedness of the children, and to create in them an ill-defined urge towards city life. (NSW Parliament 1904, p. 5)

What was seen as essential, then, was that rural teachers should be both of high quality and highly committed to their rural pupils. This was a difficult, if not intractable problem for such a centralised system. Rural schools, teachers and pupils were not quite the same as those in the cities, and this was an issue for both the selection and training of teachers:

> A proportion of bursaries is reserved for country children; they do not compete directly with city pupils. Their schools, with all their limitations, are practically as good as the urban, but their minds mature more slowly in the lonely spaces. It is later that the native ability of the country child asserts itself, in the high school, in the college, in the university. (Cole 1927, p. 39)

In 1928, a Teachers' Training College was built in Armidale – some 700 km northwest of Sydney – in order to better prepare some of those rural children as teachers expressly for rural primary schools. Its programme would differ from that at the Sydney Teachers College, still under the influence of Mackie.[4] Even here, though, the real difficulties of rural education seemed to elude educationalists. As one of the first graduates of this 'purpose built' Training College, Miss Dulcie Grey wrote tactfully to her College Principal, E.B. Newling, after her first year of teaching: 'May I suggest that those doing Infants' work be instructed and taught games and exercises, especially suitable where there is *not* a piano' (cited in Reid and Martin 2003, p. 62).

This was not the only criticism of the centralisation of the teacher education provided by the College. Turner wrote over a decade later that there was little real, sustained attention at Armidale to the realities of rural schools and teaching:

> [W]hile the College is making the efforts [...] to compensate for its comparative isolation in a country town it has not hitherto developed a characteristic curriculum of its own. A college in such a setting, having within easy reach a large number of small country schools, might well develop a curriculum largely directed towards preparing teachers for one-, two-, and three-teacher schools, since teachers of these schools still constitute the majority of teachers in the New South Wales Public school system. (Turner 1943, pp. 116–117)

But it was clear that these young teachers, in spite of their training and moral oversight by the Principal ('Pop' Newling) in Armidale, were in need of such practical support. Knibbs and Turner had noted earlier that '[t]he most serious defect of the system of education in New South Wales is the employment, as teachers, of young people of immature education, of immature physical and moral development, utterly without experience in teaching and therefore without knowledge of its scope and significance' (Cole 1927, p. 64). In South Australia, too, 'the question of academic standards' among teachers was raised:

> In 1908 there was obvious official consternation over the fact that 28 per cent of first year and 22 per cent of second-year students at the college had not passed in

any of their university subjects. It had by then become abundantly clear that the intellectual rigour of university work was beyond the capacity of a considerable number of entrants to teaching. (Hyams 1976, p. 218)

There was a growing tension between the impetus for teacher education that was to develop the intellectual and cultural attributes of the new nation's teachers and the corresponding impetus towards 'a greater emphasis on the practical aspects of their education' (Hyams 1976, p. 219). As noted at the time:

> As long as we insist on the almost Herculean task which requires our young men and women to stand up and teach a mixed class of seventy boys and girls, then culture is of little value, if they have not learned to keep those seventy boys and girls mentally active and strictly and quietly obedient. (New South Wales Parliament 1904)

Rather than emphasising teacher education as an opportunity for cultural and intellectual education for student teachers, the departmental view was that 'education in a university should not in any way be regarded as a substitute for proper professional education' (Hyams 1976, p. 220).

As noted above, when Mackie arrived to head the new Teachers' College in Sydney, the recruitment of teachers from among the ranks of pupil teachers was officially abandoned, although the practice continued, unofficially, for several decades in some Australian states, particularly in more remote and 'hard to staff' schools. Mackie's more liberal approach based on the 'New Education' was not universally admired within NSW, but his powerful position as Head of the Teachers College and subsequently Professor of Education at Sydney University meant that these ideas remained dominant within the discourse and practice of teacher education in that state for some time. This was also true in Victoria, where John Smyth held similar positions. In South Australia, by contrast, Adolf Schultz, Principal of Adelaide Teachers College, 'firmly upheld the conservative position. In 1928 he contended that a training college must deal with proven and tested methods' (Hyams 1976, p. 223). As Hyams (1976, p. 224) complained, 'the result was the perpetual flow of graduating teachers eminently suited to the requirements of tradition, preservation and continuity in school organization and curricula'.

Mackie did consider the professional or technical training of students to be important, particularly once the introduction of secondary schooling allowed the recruitment of trainee teachers from amongst those who had completed their Leaving Certificate. Once students were prohibited from entering the College on the basis of a period of pupil-teaching, they needed instead to complete their secondary education as a prerequisite for admission. However, this meant that the technical, managerial 'practical' aspects of teaching could no longer be taken for granted. As Mackie (1915, p. 8) noted, the student's 'primary schooling is largely forgotten and he [sic] has engaged in neither observation nor practice'. Mackie's prime goal, however, remained the 'education' of future teachers, not their 'training'. Indeed, by 1924, Mackie was reporting that the new Scottish regulations for teacher education required that 'all men shall be graduates before appointment', and urged raising standards for teachers in NSW, too. 'One year of preparation beyond the intermediate certificate stage is not enough; yet it is all that 60% of our young teachers get' (Mackie 1924, p. 41). It would be another half a century, however, before Mackie's aim in this regard would be realised (see also Turner 1961).

English teaching – working for the nation

'Every teacher is a teacher of English' (Newbolt, DCBE 1921). Formulated in the aftermath of the Great War and hence in the context of British national reconstruction, this proposition has resounded throughout the twentieth century in various English-speaking countries and their education systems. It has implications and relevance, however, not just for English teaching and English teachers, but also for teacher education and public schooling, as matters of practice and inquiry. Indeed it has been argued that an organic link exists, historically and institutionally, between the teacher of English – that eminently emulable subject – and the figure of the Teacher more generally (Green 1998). This suggests, in turn, that there would likely be particular value in linking English curriculum history more directly to the history of teacher education. For instance, as we have noted above, there are connections between the figure of the Teacher and the maintenance of the particular values and attitudes that the new Nation wished to emphasise and embody in its teaching force, expressly for the purposes of nation-building. There are more obvious connections to be made in relation to the importance of teachers being able to speak properly in the 'Mother Tongue', and moreover formed as exemplary 'English' subjects.

However, it is clear from the complaints and criticisms levelled at Australia's teachers in this period, that not every teacher was a *master* of English. The student teacher arriving for 'training' was certainly not always what the College would have wished to be dealing with, in doing the work of the nation. Though 'respectable' work, teaching was not well paid, and the presence of women in the teaching force meant that it was not the most desirable profession for the sons of middle-class families. Those who entered were, therefore, often the bright children of working-class families, marked by their long vowels and broad colonial accents. By 1914, for instance, Mackie had instituted a two-week school placement at the start of the student teacher's first year of training – 'not to give him practice but solely to allow the college to decide whether the student possesses enough natural capacity for teaching to make training worthwhile. It may reveal previously unnoticed defects of speech or manner or temper' (Mackie 1915, p. 8). A decade after the programmatic production of the new teacher had begun, Mackie reflected thus on the 'conditions which must be met if a competent body of teachers is to be created':

> In the first place there must be secured men and women of such native talent and endowments as will be adequate for the schooling of a democracy. [...] Still again there is the ethical problem of inspiring the teaching body with high ideals and enthusiasm for their calling. Only so can men and women be got with the personality necessary for professional and artistic work, and the recognition that their work in the last analysis is the development of civic responsibility and the shaping of a community equal to the tasks of self government. (Mackie 1915, p. 13)

Out in the schools, teachers were being asked to model and ensure that their students were speaking clearly and with appropriate intonation. The South Australian Course of Instruction and Suggestions for Teachers of 1910, for example, was clear about the 'constant struggle' of the English teacher to 'eradicate the weeds of bad habit' (*The Education Gazette* 1910).

This was a slow process, all around the nation. Nearly 20 years later, Elizabeth Skillen, Lecturer in English at Sydney Teachers' College, wrote:

> It is to be regretted that a large amount of the work required to be done, even with College classes, is quite elementary. Many of the students are not beyond the requirements of the primary School in their powers over spoken and written language and in their ability to read aloud an ordinary literary passage. ... [T]here is some weakness, somewhere, which admits of people at the end of ten years' schooling being unable to express themselves satisfactorily in the Mother tongue. Such weakness considerably handicaps the work which should be done in College. (Skillen 1927, p. 169)

Another decade and a half passed, and the problem remained. Referring to Armidale Teachers' College in 1943, Turner noted that:

> A quarter of an hour is set aside at the beginning of each day for corrective work in English, and during these periods a continuing effort is made to correcting speech defects. The College lecturer in speech training has commenced some work in speech therapy with school children in neighbouring schools. (Turner 1943, p. 116)

Teaching (into) the secondary school

As already indicated, public schooling was systematically extended from the 'primary' to the 'secondary' level over the period at issue here. This introduced a rather different problem with regard to the formal preparation and construction of the teacher. Whereas by the start of the twentieth century, when political struggles over secularity and governance had subsided, building a primary school system and its associated form of teacher education might be seen as readily straightforward, this was not the case with secondary schooling. Indeed it was far from unchallenged that the provision of secondary education was even a proper activity for the state to be engaged in.

Secondary education had been the province of the various religious denominations for quite some time, modelled in large part on the English public school, and referenced more often than not to the university. Primary schooling was developed from the bottom up, whereas secondary schooling tended to be organised from the top down, with public school provision and responsibility awkwardly placed somewhere in-between, in what eventually emerged as the junior-secondary comprehensive high school. Nonetheless, there was considerable growth in terms of state-sponsored secondary schooling, and Peter Board was to observe in 1935 that '[s]ince the federation of the Australian States, the provision of secondary education has shown a remarkable growth' (Board 1935, p. 10). As one of the principal architects of public schooling in post-Federation Australia, he specifically saw this as linked to the formation of a distinctive Australian identity, even while acknowledging that, at that particular moment, '[t]he history of the growth of a national consciousness of the Australian people has yet to be written' (Board 1935, p. 2).

According to educators at the time, the task of building an appropriate secondary teaching force quickly became evident. 'The rapid development of secondary schools under State control raised at an early stage the question of a supply of adequately trained teachers', Board wrote, and hence, '[f]rom 1905–1910, a special impetus was given to the training of teachers in all the Australian States' (Board 1935, p. 12). Mackie (1935) similarly observed that 'the training of teachers for secondary schools' was an urgent concern: 'If these schools are to provide the right upbringing for our adolescent population between the ages of twelve and eighteen years the most important task of the administrator will be to secure and appoint well qualified teachers' (Mackie 1935, p. 87). Indeed, the 'adolescent' had recently become a new object of welfare and education, with Lovell's chapter on 'Psychological and Social Characteristics of Adolescence' featuring in the same volume in which Board and Mackie were writing – Cole's (1935) edited volume *The education of the adolescent in Australia*.

Noting what was emerging as 'a policy of universal adolescent education certainly up to the age of fifteen and probably in no long time to a later age', Mackie (1935, pp. 98–99) wrote that '[t]he first necessity and the most important is to make provision for a sufficient supply of well qualified teachers'. He claimed that:

> [t]hey must be men and women with a broad outlook and clear conception of the nature and purpose of secondary education, competent in their knowledge of the branches they teach, and *possessed of the tact and sympathy needed to guide young people through the period of adolescence.* (Mackie 1935, pp. 98–99; emphasis added)

Moreover, whereas primary teacher education was from the outset characteristically a process of time-intensive and regulated study, usually residential in rural areas, and explicitly oriented towards the formation of character (Green and Reid 2002, Vick 2003), secondary teacher education was quite differently realised, as Turner noted in 1943:

> The programmes of preparation for secondary school teachers in the main follow those in operation in England, namely the completion of a degree course in a university, followed by (or taken concurrently with) a year of professional preparation either in the university or in a teachers' college. (Turner 1943, p. 231)

Knowledge, properly ratified, figured much more prominently: there were 'disciplines' and 'subjects'. There was indeed considerable faith placed in the value of a university education, as a decisive feature of the formation of the secondary school teacher. 'English' was one such subject-discipline, though we argue here and elsewhere that it was an especially significant one. This was because, as much curriculum-historical commentary now indicates, it brought together ideology and culture, language and power in a rich discursive mix (Goodson and Medway 1990, Peel *et al.* 2000, Green 2003). Board was, in fact, particularly concerned to promote the teaching of English in the new secondary education, proposing in his 'Introduction' to the 1911 NSW *Courses of Study in High Schools* that '[i]t is especially in the use of the mother tongue and the study of literature that the high school will exercise its highest influence upon the general training of pupils' (cited in Crane and Walker 1957, p. 116).

The figure of the Teacher was crucial here: a distinctive moral personage, an exemplary, emulable Subject (Hunter 1988, Green 1998). The perceived importance of English in this regard is further indicated by the fact that, notwithstanding the development of different streams or types of secondary schooling, English was central to all of them: 'In all the courses provision is made for a group of studies which is common to them all, having no immediate bearing upon vocational ends, but designed to provide for the common needs and the common training of well educated citizenship' (Crane and Walker 1957, p. 116). English was most emphatically one of those common subjects, and indeed first among them.

As might be expected, the argument of the Newbolt Report on the teaching of English in England and Wales – that the study of English should be built into the total educational experience across all stages – clearly had an impact in Australia, as elsewhere in the Empire. This is witnessed, for example, by stated views such as that of C.B. Newling, foundation Principal of Armidale Teachers College. In discussing 'efficiency in teacher training' and 'correct speech habits' in 1928, he emphasised 'the grammatical purity of the language' and urged both his lecturing staff and his student-teachers to see themselves, each and everyone, as 'a teacher of English because he is a teacher in English' (cited in Green and Reid 2002, p. 43). In a similar fashion and at much the same time, Miss Elizabeth Skillen of Sydney Teachers College, speaking to the annual conference of the Secondary Teachers' Association, observed the following:

> At Teachers' College all students preparing for Lower Primary, Rural, Domestic Science or Junior Technical School Teaching (i.e. all one or two year students) receive instruction and practice both in English and in the Teaching of English, for the college takes the view that every teacher who uses the English language as a medium of instruction should be an English teacher, though only those specially qualified should be allowed or required to handle Literature. (Skillen 1927, p. 168)

In effect all teachers, regardless of their subject area or level of teaching, would on such a view be functioning effectively as English teachers, in an important albeit generalist sense. That view remained common for much of the twentieth century, in fact, although it was variously understood and realised. Again it should be noted that the term 'English' is charged with a polysemy, here embracing at once the language and the subject, and referring to the teacher as a particular kind of especially 'qualified' person: the English teacher as 'superior being', an eminently cultured individual, and hence a special kind of personage, a Model.

At issue here is the notion of the 'fully trained', 'professional teacher', a figure that emerged steadily if in a piecemeal fashion over the course of the nineteenth century, before being formalised in the early twentieth century in Australia, in the new Teachers' Colleges. The nineteenth-century British educationalist, Kay-Shuttleworth, in his original initiative at Battersea, ushered in the modern system of teacher training, organised by his vision of a new kind of teacher–pupil relationship, forged in the classroom (Selleck 1994, pp. 137–138). There has been much debate about this figure and the forms of training and supervision that developed around it.

Making specific reference to English teaching, Patterson (2000) draws attention to the newly formed 'sympathetic teacher', formed 'within the apparatus of an increasingly secularised education system designed for "the masses" and destined to be supported by state funding' (Patterson 2000, p. 285). This can be understood in a Foucauldian fashion as a new kind of educational technology: the teacher–pupil couplet, as a highly organised and productive socio-pedagogic relationship (Hunter 1988). It is important to note here that, firstly, the student referred to in this way is both *individualised* and a *population* category, a member of an (age-)cohort, a 'class'; and secondly, that couplet must be linked to another technology, the 'text'. The result is what has been called, in fact, a 'teacher-text-pupil triplet', as a new form of social and educational management (McHoul 1988).

Learning how to operate within the terms of this relationship, in the context of the liberal classroom, and preparing student-teachers to do so, represented new challenges for teacher education, as itself a distinctive social apparatus, usefully summarised as 'a thoroughly heterogeneous ensemble consisting of discourses, institutions, architectural forms, regulatory decisions, laws, administrative measures, scientific statements, philosophical, moral and philanthropic propositions' (Foucault 1980, p. 194). The point is, however, this apparatus is called into being by the challenge of a new generational ('problem') population, which now had to be managed and marshalled into an uncertain, risky future. In Australia, this meant constructing a nation that could sustain itself and forge its own identity, even while negotiating the shifting geopolitical and cultural dynamics of the twentieth century, far from its British 'home'.

Conclusion

Teacher education expanded and diversified in the first half of the twentieth century to accommodate a burgeoning new population of school-aged children, from Kindergarten right through to Matriculation. Elementary ('primary') schooling morphed into (and then articulated with) an elaborate post-primary system. Primary teachers were the first to be brought within a fully professionalised regime, in principle at least, followed, although much less systematically, by secondary teachers. Moreover, over this period, English was conceived as the cornerstone of teaching and curriculum. Was it assumed that, somehow, a deep immersion in an academic discipline like English was as effective, in terms of the formation of teachers, as being immersed in the total environment of the Teachers College? It was clear that the former remained superior to the latter, in terms of social status – being an English scholar, licensed by the University, was more prestigious than being a College graduate. The salient point here, however, is that each form of teacher education differently but relatedly equipped the would-be teacher with appropriate forms of authority and expertise, so as to conduct him- or herself properly and effectively in the classroom, with due regard to the particular pupils they must teach. In this sense, then, there is, at the very least, an affinity between English as a distinctive subject-discipline and teacher education more generally, and between the secondary English teacher and the primary schoolteacher.

But were they good enough? *Are* they, even now? What skills are needed? What knowledges? We have already noted the persistence of a deficiency view of teachers, as well as and alongside an inflated view of their importance in preparing Australia's young people for the future and schooling the nation. Among other things, Australian teachers needed to work constantly at both self-improvement and the improvement of the accents and habits of speech and thought of the children and young people in their charge. The material that primary school children were to read remained largely focused on the British Empire rather than on their new Australia, though some shift in emphasis in this regard was apparent (Green and Cormack 2011). And their reading was clearly serving a national purpose for the ex-colony, as the following example from a school Reader indicates:

The blackfellow is a very low form of savage. He cannot learn so well as many blacks in other lands. He can count only up to five; after that number he uses a term which means 'many'. (*Victorian Reading Book*, Class II, 1905; cited in Fabian and Loh 1980, p. 125)

In setting, modelling, and practising the clear and thoughtful rendering of English, in both speech and writing ('reading'), Australian teachers, all around the continent, were helping to form the new nation in very particular ways. That 'White Australia' remained official Government policy until 1966 can to some extent be understood, now, as a reflection of how the new nation was formed, and its population schooled. As Reid and Santoro (2006, pp. 146–147) argue, it is difficult but essential to acknowledge that the White Australia Policy was built into the very foundations of the educational institutions in which a still-large proportion of Australia's present generations of educational leaders were schooled:

> Australia was still White Australia until 1972. This means that practically everyone who has in recent years held positions of power or influence or authority in education, and 'that grew up in Australia also grew up in White Australia and grew up with all the attitudes and values that White Australian stood for'. (Burney 1996, pp. 57–58)

Teacher identity, as Grosvenor and Lawn (2001) have argued in relation to England, is indeed usefully seen as intertwined with national identity. Out in the Antipodes, our forebears constructed a new Australia in a vast nation-continent whose history they chose all too often to ignore as they looked 'Home' to England, and beyond to the reassurance of the British Empire. It seems likely that the effects of those new teacher identities shaped in our first institutes for teacher education are still being felt.

Acknowledgements

We want to acknowledge our ongoing work in this regard with Phil Cormack. Much of the research drawn on here arose originally from an ARC-funded project, as part of a larger programme of curriculum-historical investigation focused largely on the late nineteenth century and the first half of the twentieth century – Bill Green, Jo-Anne Reid and Phillip Cormack, *Schooling Australia: A Curriculum History of English Teaching, Teacher Education and Public Schooling – From Federation to World War 2*, ARC Large Grant (2001–2003).

Notes

1. We refer specifically to New South Wales and South Australia. The Colleges studied were Sydney Teachers College and Armidale Teachers College in New South Wales. Further to this, and to a lesser extent, research was undertaken with regard to Adelaide Teachers College in South Australia.
2. For an account of a situation where the teachers were clearly both unprepared and lacking support, see Meadmore (2003a, 2003b) on Queensland's reform initiatives in the period in question.
3. For a similar sentiment in the UK, see Adams (1922, p. 2) on the challenge of the 'new teaching': 'Fortunately our profession is safe from the danger of violent change coming from within'.

Australian educationists like Peter Board, however, were an obvious exception in this regard. On the trope of the 'new', see Green and Cormack (2008, pp. 253–254).
4. It should be noted, however, that Mackie himself was keenly interested in the challenge for teacher education of the rural schools (Hyams 1979, p. 76).

References

Adams, J., 1922. *The new teaching*. London: Hodder & Stoughton.

Board, P., 1935. The development of secondary education in Australia. *In*: P.R. Cole, ed. *The education of the adolescent in Australia*. Melbourne: Melbourne University Press, 1–12.

Boyd, W. and Rawson, W., 1965. *The story of the new education*. London: Heinemann.

Browne, G.S., ed., 1927. *Education in Australia: a comparative study of the educational systems of the six Australian states*. London: Macmillan.

Burney, L., 1996. President's statement, NSWAECG 1995. *NSW Department of School Education Aboriginal Education Policy*. Sydney: NSW Department of School Education.

Cole, P.R., 1927. New South Wales. *In*: G.S. Browne, ed. *Education in Australia: a comparative study of the educational systems of the six Australian states*. London: Macmillan, 1–25.

Cole, P.R., ed., 1935. *The education of the adolescent in Australia*. Melbourne: Melbourne University Press.

Cormack, P., 2004. *Adolescence, schooling and English/literacy: formations of a problem in early twentieth century South Australia*. Thesis (PhD). University of South Australia.

Crane, A.R. and Walker, W.G., 1957. *Peter Board: his contribution to the development of education in New South Wales*. Melbourne: Australian Council for Educational Research.

Departmental Committee of the Board of Education (DCBE), 1921. *The teaching of English in England: being the report of the departmental committee appointed by the president of the Board of Education to inquire into the position of English in the educational system of England*. The Newbolt Report. London: HMSO.

Fabian, S. and Loh, M., 1980. *Children in Australia: an outline history*. Melbourne: Hyland House.

Foucault, M., 1980. The confession of the flesh. *In*: C. Gordon, ed. *Power/knowledge: selected interviews and other writings 1972–1977*. Brighton: Harvester Press, 195–228.

Goodson, I. and Medway, P., eds., 1990. *Bringing English to order: the history and politics of a school subject*. London: The Falmer Press.

Green, B., 1998. Born again teaching? Governmentality, 'grammar' and public schooling. *In*: T. Popkewitz and M. Brennan, eds. *Foucault's challenge: discourse, power and knowledge*. New York and London: Teachers College Press, 173–204.

Green, B., 2003. Curriculum, public education and the national imaginary: re-schooling Australia? *In*: A. Reid and P. Thomson, eds. *Towards a public curriculum*. Brisbane: PostPressed with the Australian Curriculum Studies Association, 17–32.

Green, B. and Cormack, P., 2008. Curriculum history, 'English' and the new education; or, installing the empire of English. *Pedagogy, culture and society*, 16 (3), 253–267.

Green, B. and Cormack, P., 2011. Literacy, nation, schooling: reading (in) Australia. *In*: D. Tröhler, T.S. Popkewitz, and D.F. Labaree, eds. *Schooling and the making of citizens in the long nineteenth century: comparative visions*. London and New York: Routledge, 241–261.

Green, B. and Reid, J., 2002. Constructing the teacher and schooling the nation. *History of education review*, 31 (2), 30–44.

Grosvenor, I. and Lawn, M., 2001. 'This is Who We Are and This is What We Do': teacher identity and teacher work in mid-twentieth century educational discourse. *Pedagogy, culture and society*, 9 (3), 355–370.

Hunter, I., 1988. *Culture and government: the emergence of literary education*. London: Macmillan.

Hyams, B.K., 1976. The liberal-vocational dichotomy in the preparation of primary teachers: the South Australian experience, 1875–1955. *Melbourne studies in education*, 18 (1), 209–233.

Hyams, B.K., 1979. *Teacher preparation in Australia: a history of its development from 1850 to 1950*. Hawthorn: Australian Council for Educational Research.

Jayasuriya, L., Walker, D., and Gothard, J., eds., 2003. *Legacies of white Australia: race, culture and nation*. Perth: University of Western Australia Press.

Mackie, A., 1907. The training of the teacher. *The Australian journal of education*, 15 (January), 9–10.

Mackie, A., 1915. *The training of teachers in New South Wales*. Paper read to the British Association for the Advancement of Science, Sydney, August 1914. Sydney: Government Printer.

Mackie, A., 1924. Editorial notes. *Schooling*. Sydney: NSW Government Printer, 41–42.

Mackie, A., 1935. The training of teachers and the staffing of schools. *In*: P.R. Cole, ed. *The education of the adolescent in Australia*. Melbourne: Melbourne University Press, 87–99.

McHoul, A., 1988. readingS. *In*: C. Baker and A. Luke, eds. *Towards a critical sociology of reading pedagogy: papers of the XII world congress on reading*. Amsterdam and Philadelphia, PA: John Benjamins Publishing, 191–210.

McRae, C.R. and Turner, I.S., 1943. Teacher training in New South Wales. *The forum of education*, II (2), 1–15.

Meadmore, P., 2003a. The 'willing' and the 'able': a case study of curriculum reform in the early 20th century. *History of education review*, 32 (1), 16–33.

Meadmore, P., 2003b. The introduction of the 'new education' in Queensland, Australia. *History of education quarterly*, 43 (3), 372–392.

New South Wales Parliament, 1904. *Inquiry into certain educational issues.* Joint volumes of papers presented to the legislative council and legislative assembly. Sydney: NSW Government Printer.

Patterson, A., 2000. Australia: questions of pedagogy. *In*: R. Peel, A. Patterson, and J. Gerlach, eds. *Questions of English: ethics, aesthetics, rhetoric and the formation of the subject in England, Australia and the United States*. London and New York: Routledge, 233–300.

Peel, R., Patterson, A., and Gerlach, J., 2000. *Questions of English: ethics, aesthetics, rhetoric and the formation of the subject in England, Australia and the United States*. London and New York: Routledge.

Reid, J. and Martin, S., 2003. 'Speak softly, be tactful, and assist cheerfully...' Women beginning teachers in 1930s NSW. *Change: transformations in education*, 6 (1), 48–69.

Reid, J. and Santoro, N., 2006. Cinders in snow? Indigenous teacher identities in formation. *Asia-Pacific journal of teacher education*, 34 (2), 143–160.

Rizvi, F., 1997. Beyond the east-west divide: education and the dynamics of Australia-Asia relations. *Australian educational researcher*, 24 (1), 13–26.

Saunders, G., 1976. One hundred years of teacher education in South Australia. Lecture delivered at Adelaide College of Advanced Education on Friday, 4 June. *In*: *A collection of centenary papers*. Adelaide: Adelaide College of Advanced Education 1976–1976 Archives, 5–15.

Selleck, R.J.W., 1968. *The new education: the English background 1870–1914*. Melbourne: Pitman & Sons.

Selleck, R.J.W., 1982. State education and culture. *Australian journal of education*, 26 (1), 3–19.

Selleck, R.J.W., 1994. *James Kay-Shuttleworth: journey of an outsider*. Ilford: The Woburn Press.

Skillen, E., 1927. The teaching of English in teachers' college. *Schooling*, X (5), 168–175.

Spaull, A., 1998. Public education in Australia: an historical essay. *In*: A. Reid, ed. *Going public: education policy and public education in Australia*. Adelaide: Australian Curriculum Studies Association, 3–8.

The Education Gazette, 1910. Course of instruction and suggestions to teachers [online]. *The Education Gazette*, 23 February, pp. 46–57. Available from: http://unisa.aquabrowser.com/?q=The+Gazette+Course+of+Study+1907 [Accessed 12 August 2012].

Theobald, M., 1990. Women's teaching labour, the family and the state in nineteenth-century Victoria. *In*: M.R. Theobald and R.J.W. Selleck, eds. *Family, school and state in Australian history*. Sydney: Allen & Unwin, 25–44.

Turner, I.S., 1943. *The training of teachers in Australia: a comparative and critical survey*. ACER Research Series No. 61. Melbourne: Melbourne University Press.

Turner, I.S., 1961. The professional preparation of teachers in Australia. *Melbourne studies in education 1959–1960*. Melbourne: Melbourne University Press, 1–45.

Vick, M., 2003. Building 'professionalism' and 'character' in the single-purpose teachers colleges, 1900–1950. *Australian journal of teacher education*, 28 (1), 40–50.

Whitehead, K. and Wilkinson, L., 2008. Teachers, policies and practices: a historical review of literacy teaching in Australia. *Journal of early childhood literacy*, 8 (1), 7–24.

Reflections: continuing the conversation

Maxine Stephenson

Faculty of Education, The University of Auckland, Auckland, New Zealand

Introduction

An overarching methodological focus in this issue of the *Journal of Educational Administration and History* has been to engage Michel Foucault's concern with 'a history of the present'. I was, therefore, prompted to begin my overview of the collection *in* the present – specifically, and in keeping with the topic for this special issue, with a comment on the way the 'education, youth, nation' nexus is expressed in this historical moment, that is, in education for global citizenship. This I believed would allow me to read in the articles what entities, expectations or actions might be 'presupposed by current practices ... [that] in ways we don't realize, are rooted in the past' (Rajchman 1985, p. 4). It would also enable me to reach further back to see what echoes of earlier pasts might be captured within the issues discussed in the articles and that continue to impact today.

Globalisation is now a well-rehearsed theme in social science research. Theoretical sophistication in the field has increasingly focused on the history of globalising processes over a number of dimensions, and on local, national and regional dynamics in these processes (Dale 2008). As education is now being called on to prepare citizens who are able to contemplate and contribute to the mediation of problems that are beyond the scope of the nation-state, attention to models of global citizenship in education has dominated the twenty-first-century landscape. The 2002 introduction of citizenship education into the national curriculum for secondary schools in the UK, for example, has focused on social and moral responsibility, community involvement and political literacy (Ofsted 2006). In Australia, secondary school students are to gain 'the knowledge, skills, values and dispositions of active and informed citizenship' at national, regional and international levels (DEEWR 2012). Reflecting global governance arrangements (Dale 2008), we are witnessing also an increasing role for international non-governmental organisations in the task. As I write from New Zealand, three interactive global citizenship education workshops are being planned for teachers so that they may support New Zealand youth engagement and participation both in the classroom and as prospective delegates for an international Model United Nations conference.

According to Schattle (2008), there is little agreement as to what global citizenship is. Certainly as a policy direction for education, it has received mixed responses, some scepticism as to its purpose, and variable commitment. In a volume that draws together contributions from many national contexts, Openshaw and White (2005, p. 10) suggest that '[w]e preach rather than practice democracy and citizenship, especially in our schools'. They question the implications of this traditionally conservative approach and argue for a critical global conception of citizenship and democracy rather than an uncritical acceptance of its principles. What remnants of the past might remain alive in, and continue to inform, these responses and the concerns that they raise? What threads of the intent encapsulated in the notion of education of youth for global citizenship might be discernible within the articles in this issue? What might they tell us of the contingencies, interconnections, potentialities and possibilities that could help make sense of this policy direction in the present?

Citizenship and empire

The linking of citizenship, politics and law harks back to enlightenment philosophy and is articulated through an understanding of the social contract – the agreement through which people become citizens. Underpinned by a commitment to socially agreed morals, values and ethical norms, this social agreement recognises the rights and freedom of individuals within a community, although in essence it is an expression of the collective will. For otherwise self-interested individuals, it enables pursuit of the common good or public interest (Rousseau 1762/1953). In a comprehensive cross-national analysis, Green (1990) demonstrates convincingly how modern education systems have been implicated in securing the conditions that make such an agreement possible through 'the formation of ideologies and collective beliefs which legitimate state power and underpin concepts of nationhood and national "character"' (p. 77).

As some of the contributors to this issue demonstrate, there is nothing new in notions of citizenship that reference to links beyond national borders, except, perhaps, in the language which defines them. This is part of the entanglement that accompanies a colonial past. There is also nothing surprising about the varying responses to the imperial 'home' that were being expressed more than a century into the relationship, in an Australia of newly united but firmly ensconced state systems. Central to Phil Cormack's analysis of the first account of schooling 'across the nation', for example, is the understanding that appropriately educated adolescents were a source of hope for a *nation* under threat – the future citizens of a white 'British nation in the south'. This, he suggests, was a complex amalgam of the nation's physical location, eugenic thought within the 'white' world and the increasing reference to new scientific and social knowledges and expertise. Julie McLeod's Mr K. Cromo, on the other hand, whilst certainly demonstrating awareness of the citizen of the world, was scathing of the possible intrusion of the 'stilted Englishmen or cosmopolitans' in the shaping of Australian national identity. And this despite, or perhaps because of (and in a foreshadowing of twenty-first-century initiatives), his wider call for tolerance and justice. Nonetheless, McLeod explains, civics education at the time expressed what would become a version of a later refrain where an anticipated 'internationalist outlook' for some would sit uncomfortably with a presupposed denial of possibility for Others.

For Bill Green and Jo-Anne Reid, the teacher of the early 1900s was a key figure in creating a very specific kind of nation, one that reasserted the transnational reach to the empire and who strove to maintain the integrity of the English language, both written and spoken. This was no easy feat, it would appear, according to evidence from an international meeting in London of teachers from various parts of the empire. In a programme entitled 'English language and literature: The pronunciation of English', the topic was raised and comparisons were made with the colonial neighbour, New Zealand:

> Mr L.A. Adamson (Association of Secondary Teachers of Victoria) was interested to hear Mr Firth say that the English in Victoria was not as bad as that in New South Wales. All he could say was that he was very sorry for New South Wales...He considered the most perfect English he had ever heard was among the Maoris. They had, however, naturally beautiful voices to begin with. He found all through New Zealand that the accent was something to be admired. Several people to whom he spoke on the subject agreed with Mr Firth that there was a falling off, which they attributed to importations from Australia.[1]

Examination of the context in which these conferences were initiated, and of those responsible for initiating them, casts some shadows of understanding on the complexities of what 'being British', or 'being part of the British Empire' meant in different colonial contexts, as well as in the imperial 'home' (Stephenson 2010). By the early 1900s, wider recognition of the negative connotations of empire was challenging celebratory interpretations of imperial expansion. In response, a number of aristocratic and upper-middle-class 'imperialist propaganda societies' (Bush 2000, p. 2) were being established with a view to creating greater unity and sustainability. With its founding in 1901, the League of the Empire held conferences on imperial education that brought together representatives of Education Departments and Education Institutes throughout the empire 'for the broad principle of co-operation in education' (Pollard 1912, p. 13). As Whitehead (2007) explains and demonstrates, this did not mean that there was a coherent formal policy for British imperial education. In fact, there was a degree of ambivalence amongst officials at the Board of Education at Whitehall and the Colonial Office, as well as uncertainty amongst Education Departments within the colonies and dominions about what imperial education was and/or should be. It did, however, provide the occasion for visits abroad and meetings of minds around educational problems and issues. Reflecting issues raised in the contributions by Green and Reid, Wright and Cormack, delegates from the various Australian states to the 1927 conference submitted topics for discussion relating to courses in general science in the lower sections of higher schools; the various types of secondary schools necessary for pupils between 12 and 18 and associated vocational guidance; the relationship of trade and technical training to secondary education provided, and the training of teachers for different types of school.[2]

The politics of biology

If the general thrust of formal and informal education in the early 1900s sought to inspire loyalty to and admiration for the British in taking up the 'imperial burden' and in bringing peace, happiness and prosperity throughout the empire (Milner 1913, Bush 2000), as Cormack and McLeod demonstrate, messages implicit in the language of 'burden, patriotism, service and inherent racial difference' would serve to legitimate eugenically based racist attitudes and practices. This would define the limits and possibilities for some potential citizens and ensure the physical exclusion of 'undesirable Others'. The eugenically inspired reach would not end there, however, and as Wright and Cormack convincingly argue, the development of new social knowledge in the hands of knowledge-bearing elites would provide a new means of mediating the social needs, demands, problems and dilemmas associated with the production of the most 'socially efficient', well-adjusted and well-prepared young people possible for their transition to adulthood.

Eugenicists were particularly influential in the early years of the twentieth century throughout Australia, New Zealand, Canada, England and America, during which time they were to exert considerable pressure for government recognition of their concerns. Supported by their powerful political allies and experts in the fields of medicine, psychiatry, psychology, statistics, criminology and social work, they drew on and moulded knowledge produced within the biological sciences to produce a new discourse of racial fitness. Although criticised for running counter to individual liberty, eugenic principles became increasingly supported in scientific circles, and it was those eugenicists who served as public officials and whose scientific and professional expertise combined to legitimate their position, who were to the fore in seeing realised a number of restrictive legislative measures, many centred on schooling (Snow 1990, Stephenson 1998).

In New Zealand, the most influential advocate of eugenic principles was politician and surgeon, Dr W.A. Chapple, who published, with the endorsement of some notable medical and political figures, a work which sought to bring to public attention the disturbing decline in birth rate and what he identified as the associated problem of 'the fertility of the unfit' (Chapple 1903). Besides suggesting possible solutions to this problem, this work considered the role (and right) of the state to intervene. Chapple's work demonstrates with clarity the salience of the argument that certain technologies of control become possible within a particular set of circumstances. His arguments addressed a number of concerns being expressed in New Zealand at the time and, therefore, appealed to diverse sectors of the community. Many of the issues raised in his work are central to the arguments presented by the scholars in this special issue. In his introduction, Chapple drew the reader's attention to the Darwinian-based argument of the survival of the fittest which, besides providing justification for colonisation by a dominant imperial power, with the increasing ascendancy of a dominant middle class in New Zealand and with the apparent imminent demise of Māori as a distinct group, had become a legitimating ideology for the relative success of one group over the other (Stephenson 1998).

Chapple's introductory reflection on 'criminal inheritance', positing crime as a 'natural' function of mental and physical differences, resonated with the increasing 'moral panic' about conditions emanating from the growth of the urban sector and offered ideological support for the establishment of middle-class cultural hegemony (Stephenson 1998). He identified 'the criminal, the pauper, the idiot and imbecile, the lunatic, the drunkard, the deformed, and diseased' as 'the fit man's burden', striking chords with considerable indignation being expressed by many towards increased taxation and welfare provision for the undeserving, incorrigible poor (Chapple 1903, p. xii). By providing statistical evidence of the escalating ratio of the population 'dependent upon the State, or on public or private support' (p. xiv), he posited new questions for a state becoming increasingly concerned with national efficiency and with the quality of the population as a national resource, challenging the outcomes of previous humanitarian-based charitable or state initiatives as perpetuating national degeneracy rather than as alleviating individual suffering.

Chapple (1903, p. 10) gained attention also with his identification of '[b]irths, deaths, and migration' as 'the factors which make up the population question'. The intention to restrict immigration, particularly of people of Chinese origin, was strongly debated in parliament from the 1870s and this was yet another issue for which Chapple's treatise was able to provide scientific 'proof' on which anti-alien sentiments and lobbying could be legitimated. Finally, his arguments appealed to the professional sector of the emerging middle class who, as pointed out by Shuker (1987, p. 52), were attempting 'to stake out areas of expertise and authority so that, while dealing with perceived social problems, they were also engaged in enhancing their own status, power and security'.

New education

Education, Green (1990, p. 80) claimed:

> helped construct the very subjectivities of citizenship, justifying the ways of the state to the people and the duties of the people to the state. ... [It] formed the responsible citizen, the diligent worker, the willing tax-payer, the reliable juror, the conscientious parent, the dutiful wife, the patriotic soldier and the dependable and deferential voter.

These qualities identified by Green in relation to developing systems are echoed for the 1930s 'good citizen' of McLeod's analysis. This was an era of rapid change, though, especially in terms of exposure to international events and developments, both internal and external to education. Ideas of civics and citizenship education that were tested seemed so diverse it would appear that there would be little today that does not have some veil of familiarity.

This was a heady time for education in the Antipodes, as captured in all of the articles. With the New Education Fellowship gatherings, it appeared that Australia and New Zealand were joining the big players. And they were going to maximise their opportunities from the experience. Writing of his trip to New Zealand, Mr G.T. Hankin of the English Board of Education commented: 'Everybody is astounded at the numbers. The whole business reminds one rather of a religious revival'.[3] This was a time when educationalists around the world were increasingly developing and sharing ideas through professional networks. They were of psychological, philosophical and professional matters, all of which were reflected in the establishment of new support, pedagogical and teacher education structures and all of which had significant implications for the adolescent as a citizen in the making. Katie Wright's guidance programmes saw an extended role for testing and classification in pursuit of individual happiness, social efficiency, and no 'wastage' of human potential. The new knowledge would make a new socially useful and self-aware citizen. In that secondary education was required to cater for the needs and interests of a much more diverse group of students, its role had taken on a broader application. Pre-service training was not simply a matter of providing sufficient teachers to front classes, but also of recruiting for the wide variety of courses which were to be offered to a broad student body. Bill Green and Jo-Anne Reid's new secondary teacher of the 1930s would require greater training and disciplinary education to cater to Phil Cormack's new and differentiated secondary school population, but the expectation that he/she would be of moral character and would model exemplary English language and culture would remain constant.

But what of the aboriginal child in this differentiated system? Australian Historian of Education, Dianne Snow (1989, p. xi) suggests that whilst its history had been uneven, by the 1920s 'studenthood had become the major social relation which defined youth in New South Wales'. Studenthood, she claimed, is a shifting notion, taking on different meanings in different times and spaces and according to 'class, race, gender and age'. As has been argued throughout this commentary, notions of citizenship are similarly unstable, perhaps most starkly demonstrated through McLeod's observations about the representation of Aboriginal children at the 1936 Hawaiian conference 'Education in Pacific Countries' as 'non-citizen'. I now want to step aside from that context to consider what was happening for Māori students in New Zealand during the progressive era.

The progressive ideal of incorporating the child's world into their learning was also at the heart of the adaptation policy that was introduced into the New Zealand Native Schools in the 1930s. These schools had been in place since 1867, and the shift in policy was prompted by a number of converging factors. In the first instance, concerns were being expressed by a group of professional young Māori about the impact of schooling in marginalising their cultural and political rights. These young men identified themselves as 'The Association for the Amelioration of the Maori Race' and sought to act as a cultural bridge between the state and the community (Stephenson 2008). The shift in direction was also impacted by a new policy that had been developed by the British Colonial Office for the education of 'native' populations in Tropical West Africa, itself being referenced to the Phelps Stokes Report from the USA. This in turn reflected the increasing interest in 'culture' that had been generated by the anthropologists (Simon 1998).

More significantly, perhaps, the newly appointed chief inspector of Native Schools, Douglas Ball had been taught by an ex-pupil of John Dewey, a key proponent of the educational philosophy. Ball even incorporated Dewey's writings into the Native School teachers' column in the nation's *Education Gazette*. He explained his rationale for the new policy. Teaching in the Native Schools up to that point, he said, had been of symbol – the artificial framework of our culture – and it had failed Māori in their critical period of adjustment. The school had been 'in the pa [Māori village], but not of the pa' (Ball 1940, p. 278). Whilst in retrospect Ball acknowledged the limitations of this policy as just another form of assimilation (Stephenson 2008), according to Hirini Mead, as time progressed, the Native Schools shifted from being simply 'a tool of government policy' to become 'a mixture of Maori aspirations for [their] own future and government designs for building a nation dominated by British culture, laws and institutions' (Mead 1998, pp. viii, xi). Colonisation and its shadows are felt in various ways. It would be several more decades before significant decisions such as the 1967 referendum and the 1992 Mabo decision began to redefine citizenship for Aboriginal people in Australia.

Conclusion

The articles in this issue present young people as various forms of a problem for the state, society, family or self in the first four decades of the twentieth century. As developing citizens in a liberal democracy, they were thinking individuals with rights and responsibilities, but they were also dependent, to be protected and regulated by their parents or the state. Compulsory education provided a site of conformity and the nurturing of citizenship beliefs and values. It was also a site of moral regulation, especially if a young person's needs to be controlled were framed within a discourse of parental neglect. Schools were thus sites of potential redemption, but they could also be sites of ruin. Broadening access to secondary schooling would ensure that the freedom of young people growing up would be in some way contained, keeping them occupied and out of trouble. Young people would come to attention if they were not engaging with school, or with their subjects, or if they were unable to cope with school tasks. One answer to the problem would be in providing appropriate guidance and support. Another would be in providing increasingly differentiated provision. As such, young people became objects of new scientific knowledge and expertise, to be divided up for classification and measurement, and for assignment to appropriate places of correction or guidance.

The contributions to the issue also provide important insights into how, within particular historical periods, and reflecting the socio-political circumstances peculiar to those periods, these specific modes of understanding young people and the nature, form and function of schooling were linked to meanings of citizenship and the ideal citizen. These historically contingent meanings continue to resonate today.

Notes

1. Report of the [First] Imperial Conference of Teachers' Associations convened by the League of the Empire, 13 to 17 July 1912 at the Caxton Hall, Westminster. National Archives, UK/Kew. ED 121/50 The League of the Empire 1907 IEC.
2. National Archives, UK/Kew. ED 24/2126 Imperial Education Conference 1927.
3. 27 July 1937, from Hankin to Richardson. National Archives, UK/Kew. ED 121/62 Australian Council for Educational Research: NEF 1937.

References

Ball, D.G., 1940. Maori education. *In*: I.L.G. Sutherland, ed. *The Maori people today: a general survey*. Wellington: New Zealand Institute of International Affairs and The New Zealand Council for Educational Research, 269–306.

Bush, J., 2000. *Edwardian ladies and imperial power*. Leicester, UK: Leicester University Press.

Chapple, W.A., 1903. *The fertility of the unfit*. Melbourne, Christchurch, Wellington, Dunedin and London: Whitcombe and Tombs.

Dale, R., 2008. Globalisation and education in Aotearoa/New Zealand. *In*: V. Carpenter, et al., eds. *Nga Kaupapa here: connections and contradictions in education*. South Melbourne: Cengage Learning, 25–35.

DEEWR (Department of Education, Employment and Workplace Relations), 2012. *Civics and citizenship education* [online]. Available from: http://www.civicsandcitizenship.edu.au/cce/global_citizenship_-_student_investigations,21210.html [Accessed 20 May 2012].

Green, A., 1990. *Education and state formation: the rise of education systems in England, France and the USA*. London: Macmillan.

Mead, H.M., 1998. He kupu whakataki: foreword. *In*: J. Simon, ed. *Nga kura Maori: the native schools system 1867–1969*. Auckland: Auckland University Press, viii–xi.

Milner, A., 1913. *The nation and the empire*. London: Constable.

Ofsted, 2006. *Towards consensus: citizenship in secondary schools* [online]. London: Office for Standards in Education. Available from: http://www.ofsted.gov.uk/resources/towards-consensus-citizenship-secondary-schools [Accessed 26 May 2012].

Openshaw, R. and White, C., 2005. Democracy at the crossroads? *In*: C. White and R. Openshaw, eds. *Democracy at the crossroads: international perspectives on critical global citizenship education*. Lanham, MD: Lexington Books, 3–11.

Pollard, A.F., ed., 1912. *The British Empire: its past, its present, and its future*. London: League of the Empire.

Rajchman, J., 1985. *Michel Foucault: the freedom of philosophy*. New York: Columbia University Press.

Rousseau, J.J., 1762/1953. *The social contract*. London: Penguin (1953 ed.). Translated and introduced by Maurice Cranston.

Schattle, H., 2008. *The practices of global citizenship*. Lanham, MD: Rowman & Littlefield.

Shuker, R., 1987. *The one best system?* Palmerston North: Dunmore Press.

Simon, J., 1998. Anthropology, native schooling and Maori: the politics of 'cultural adaptation' policies. *Oceania*, 68 (1), 61–78.

Snow, D.S., 1989. *The state, youth and schooling: the social construction of studenthood in New South Wales 1788–1948* [online]. Thesis (PhD). School of Learning Studies, University of Wollongong. Available from: http://ro.uow.edu.au/theses/2026 [Accessed 9 June 2012].

Snow, D.S., 1990. Historicising the integration debate. *Australasian Journal of Special Education*, 13 (2), 28–38.

Stephenson, M.S., 1998. Eugenics and the shaping of citizens. *In*: I. McLaren, et al., eds. *Voice, vision and identity in history of education, 2*. Auckland: Australian and New Zealand History of Education Society, 447–464.

Stephenson, M.S., 2008. Education, state and society: an historical analysis. *In*: V. Carpenter, et al., eds. *Nga Kaupapa here: connections and contradictions in education*. South Melbourne: Cengage Learning, 1–10.

Stephenson, M.S., 2010. Learning about empire and the imperial education conferences in the early twentieth century: creating cohesion or demonstrating difference? *History of education review*, 39 (2), 24–35.

Whitehead, C., 2007. The concept of British education policy in the colonies 1850–1960. *Journal of educational administration and history*, 39 (2), 161–173.

Index

Note: Page numbers in **bold** type refer to figures
Page numbers in *italic* type refer to tables
Page numbers followed by 'n' refer to notes

ability: grouping 44; mental 44
Aborigines 70; adolescence 72; children 8, 71, 72; children's intelligence 72–3; education 68, 70–1; students 60
Adams, J. 94
Adamson, L.A. 101
Adelaide: University of 79
Adelaide Teachers' College 87
adolescence 8, 13, 15–16; Aboriginal children 72; and race 16–20; racialised discourse 22–3; sub-populations 22
adolescent citizen 57–73
agencies: education 51
Anderson, F. 79
Argus, The 69
Armidale Teachers' College 86, 89, 91
Arnold, M. 27
Asia: immigration 82
assessment 31, 45
Australasian Association for the Advancement of Science 38, 41
Australian Association for Research in Education 6; conference (2010) 6
Australian Council for Educational Research (ACER) 38, 59
Australian Fellowship of Education conference (1937) 68
Australian Institute of Industrial Psychology (AIIP) 45
Australian National Research Council 69
Australian Teacher 61

Bagley, W. 24
Baker, B. 14, 17, 32n
Ball, D. 105
Benjamin, J. 58
Bessant, J. 19, 31
Binet, A. 39

biology: politics of 102–3
Board, P. 83, 90, 91
bodies: health 28
Bovet, P. 67–8, 73
Boyd, W. 67; and Rawson, W. 83
Brehony, K. 2
Britain 36; Colonial Office 105; colonies 81; educational reform 82; educationalists 82; imperial education 101–2; National Institute for Industrial Psychology 45; national reconstruction 88
Browne, G.S. 15, 20, 26–7, 29, 80, 82, 85; *Education in Australia: a comparative study of the educational systems of the six Australian states* 7, 13–15, 21, 22
Burt, C. 30

California: University of 67
Cameron, R.G. 39
Campbell, C.: and Sherington, G. 74
caring discourses 32n
Carnegie Corporation 59
Carnegie Council on Adolescent Development: *Turning Points* (1989) 19
central schools 24; new 27
Chapple, W.A. 1–3, 102–3
children: Aborigine 8, 71, 72–3; guidance 40, 46–9, 50, 51; guidance clinics 47, 48; post-primary in early twentieth-century 13–32
citizen: adolescent 57–73
citizenship 28, 58–9, 67; adolescent education 8, 61, 65; and empire 100–2; good citizens 8; learning 8; new citizen 8; studies of 58
civics 60; education 60–4, 101
Civics in Australian schools (Hoy) 61–2
Clarapède, E. 29
class: middle 103; social 22; working 22
classification 52

INDEX

clear-thinking 58
clinics: child guidance 47, 48
Clubb, W. 22, 27, 28
Cole, P.R. 20, 21, 22, 26, 29, 30, 83–4; *The education of the adolescent in Australia* 2, 90
colonialism 105; discourses 68
colonies: British 81
Columbia University 35–6
Commonwealth Fund 46, 47
competence: teachers 89
competitiveness 28
compulsory education 21, 106
compulsory schooling 6; post-primary 7
confinement: institutional 32n
Cormack, P. 6–7, 13–32, 100–1, 102
cosmopolitanism: localism and schooling adolescent citizen (interwar) 57–73
criminal inheritance 103
Cromo, K. 58, 101
cultural hegemony 103
culture 26–8, 31; expectations 72
Cumulative School History cards 42
Cunningham, K. 38, 39, 65
curriculum 3, 62–3

Davey, C. 29
degeneration 17
delinquent practices 42
democracy 63; education 63–4; liberal 106; schooling 66
Depression 44
development stages 29–30
Dewey, J. 105
difference 63; individual 38, 39
discourses: caring 32n; colonialism 68; of educational change 5; internationalism 68
dispositif 7, 23, 31
drifting 41

Education of the adolescent in Australia, The (Cole) 2, 90
Education in Australia: a comparative study of the educational systems of the six Australian states (Browne) 7, 13–15, 31; South Australia chapter headings 20
Education for Complete Living: The Challenge of Today conference (1937) 8, 64–8; NEF principles 66
Education Gazette and Teachers' Aid 42–3, 46
Education (of Native Races) in Pacific Countries conference (Hawaii 1936) 8, 57, 59, 68–73, 105; race 69–70; topics 69
educational ladder 26
Educational Psychology 28–30, 31
educator's basic assumption 70
efficiency: social 46
Elkin, A.P. 69, 70–1, 72–3

empire: and citizenship 100–2
English 9, 81, 91; curriculum history 88; immersion in 93; literature 27; pronunciation 101; -speaking countries 88; teaching 88–9
English Board of Education 104
Englishness 9, 80, 81
Ensor, B. 64–5
ethical judgement 67
eugenicists 9, 102
eugenics movement 9, 19, 30, 31
evidence-based practices 31
expectations: culture 72

feeblemindedness 39
Fellowship of Education 69
Fellowship of Education: education for complete living conference (1937) 8, 64–8
feminism: theory 6
Finland 66
fitness 28, 31
Foucault, M. 5–6, 15, 23, 60, 92, 99; *dispositif* 7, 23, 31

genealogy 4–10
Geneva: University of 67–8
Giles, G.R. 42, 44
globalisation 99
governmentality 5
Great Chain of Being 16–17
Great South Land 81
Great War 88
Green, A. 100, 104
Green, B. 101; and Reid, J-A. 8–9, 33, 79–94, 101, 104
Grey, D. 86
Grosvenor, I.: and Lawn, M. 80, 94
Grosz, E. 6
Groves, W. 69
guidance 37–49; child 40, 46–9, 50, 51; educational 40–6, 50, 51; movement in interwar Australia 35–52; NSW 44; promise of 49–51; schooling 7; vocational 7, 40, 40–6, 50, 51
guidance clinics: child 47, 48

Hadow Report (1931) 18–19
Hales, N. 45
Hall, G.S. 17, 29–30
Halpin, D. 4
Hankin, G.T. 104
Hansen, P. 18
happiness 46
Hart, F.W. 67
health: bodies 28; mental 47; preventative care 47; preventative initiatives 46
hegemony: cultural 103
high school system 21

INDEX

history 4–10, 61
History of Education Review 5
history of the present 5
Holbrook, A. 42, 51
Hoy, A. 61–3; *Civics in Australian schools* 61–2; *Teaching of history and civics in Victorian secondary schools* report (1934) 62
Hyams, B.K. 87

identity 90; national 58, 101; teachers 80, 94
immigration 1–3, 82
imperial education 101–2
individualised education 49–51
indoctrination 67
industrial psychology 46
inheritance: criminal 103
institutions: confinement 32n
intelligence scale 39
intelligence tests 29, 38; psychology 71
internationalism: discourses 68
intervention 46, 47, 52

J J Rousseau Institute for Educational Sciences 68
Johnson, J.A. 38
Johnson, L.: and Tyler, D. 5
Journal of Educational Administration and History 99
Journal of inspectors of schools of Australia, The 62
judgement: ethical 67

Kay-Shuttleworth, J. 93
Keesing, F. 59, 70, 74; *Education in Pacific Countries* conference (1936) 69
Knibbs, G.: and Turner, J. 83, 86
knowledge 91; psychological 51

Lawn, M.: and Grosvenor, I. 80, 94
League of the Empire 101
League of Nations 59; research activities 68; Schools' Day (1932) 62
learning: citizenship 8
Lesko, N. 16–17
Lewis, J. 39
liberal democracy 106
Liberal Education 27, 31
localism 57–73
London 101
Lovell, H.T. 19, 90

McCallum, D. 28
McKellar, D. 82–3
Mackie, A. 84, 87–8, 89, 90
McLellan, R. 57–8
McLeod, J. 8, 57–73, 101, 102; and Wright, K. 1–10

McRae, C.R.: and Turner, I.S. 85, 86
McRae, J. 42, 43
Māori 10; rights 105
Martin, A.H. 45
Mead, H. 105
Meadmore, P. 94
Melbourne 47
Melbourne Teachers' College 39
mental ability 44
mental capacity 29
mental hygiene 31; councils 47
mentally defective 21
Meredyth, D.: and Thomas, J. 58
middle class 103
Minnesota: University of 36
misfits 37–40, 43
Mitchell, W. 79
modern education systems 100
Montessori, M. 64–5
Mosely Educational Commission (1904) 16

Nangle, J. 41, 52
National Assessment Program - Literacy and Numeracy (NAPLAN) 3
national identity 58, 101
nationalism 80
Native Schools 10, 105
New Education 72, 82, 83, 84, 87; teachers 84
New Education Fellowship (NEF) 50, 63, 65, 104; Education for Complete Living conference (1937) 8, 64–8; research activities 68
New Era in Education 63, 65
New South Wales (NSW) 20, 21, 22; *Courses of Study in High Schools* (1911) 91; Department of Public Instruction 41; education defects 86; educational system 83; guidance 44; Legislative Council and Assembly, Pastoral and Agricultural Subcommittee 85; Parliament 84; Royal Commission 83; School Counselling Service 48; School Medical Service 48; teacher education 85
New Zealand 9–10, 99–100, 102–3; educational history 9; English pronunciation 101; middle class 103; Native Schools 10, 105
Newbolt Report on the teaching of English in England and Wales (1921) 91
Newling, C.B. 86, 91
normality 52

Openshaw, R.: and White, C. 100
optimism 3–4

Patterson, A. 92
physically afflicted 21
politics of biology 102–3
Popkewitz, T.S. 63–4

INDEX

populations: management distances 26
post-colonial progressivism 59
post-primary child: in early twentieth-century 13–32
post-primary education 6
post-primary schooling 6, 7, 14, 31
practices: evidence-based 31
primary schooling 87–8, 90; extensions 26
problems: in education 15, 16; rural 85; 12–15 age 21, 22, 26–7, 30
progressivism 73; education 9; ideals 66; post-colonial 59
projects: reform 23–30
psy 51
psychological knowledge 51
psychological sciences 30
psychological tests 41
psychology 29, 37–40, 51, 52; classifications 71; industrial 46; intelligence testing 71; new 37
psychometric testing 45
puberty 72
public education 14
Public Instruction Act (1880) 85
public schooling 8
pupil teacher 83–4
Putland, F. 61

qualified teachers 90
quality: teachers 8

race 15; adolescence 16–20; discourse 22–3
racial capacity 71
racial prejudice 72
racialism 16
Rawson, W.: and Boyd, W. 83
record cards 43
reform projects: new and old 23–30
Reid, J-A.: and Green, B. 8–9, 33, 79–94, 101, 104; and Santoro, N. 94
responsibility: social 58
Review of Education in Australia (1938) 49
Richardson, J.G. 32n
rights: Māori 105
Rose, N. 29, 30, 46, 51
Rural Problem 85

Samson, P.G. 18
Santoro, N.: and Reid, J. 94
Saunders, G. 80
Schattle, H. 100
scholarship: education 5–6
School Counselling Service 44
school placement: two-week 88
schools/schooling 60, 80, 100–1; central schools 24, 27; citizenship 66; compulsory 6; compulsory post-primary 7; counsellor network 44; democracy 66; efficiency 24; English secondary 89–93; guidance 7; high school system 21; Native Schools 10, 105; post-primary 6, 7, 14, 31; primary 87–8, 90; primary school extensions 26; public 8; Scotland 18; secondary education 89–93; special schools 21; superior schools 26; technical 24; universal 31; Victoria 18; vocational 21, *see also* teachers
Schulz, A.J. 14, 20, 22, 24, 28, 87
science 27, 28–30, 31–2; psychological 30
Scotland: school systems 18
secondary schools: English 89–93; teachers 91
Secondary Teachers' Association 92
self-insight 49
self-understanding 49
Selleck, R.J.W. 82
Shalit, M. 47
Sherington, G.: and Campbell, C. 74
Shuker, R. 103
Skillen, E. 39, 89, 91–2
Smith, S.H. 42
Snow, D. 104–5
social class 22
social efficiency 23–6, 31
social responsibility 58
social status 93
South Africa 65
South Australia 28; academic standards 86–7; Course of Instruction and Suggestions for Teachers of 1910 89; education 29; education conspectus **25**; teachers 81
Special Education 32n
special schools 21
status: social 93
Stephenson, M. 9–10, 99–106
studenthood 105
students: Aborigine 60; cosmopolitanism 73
Sturtevant, S. 35–6, 49
subjectivity 51
superior schools 26
Sydney 21
Sydney Morning Herald 60; misfits 39–40
Sydney Teachers' College 39, 86, 89, 91–2
Sydney University 45, 69, 84
sympathetic teacher 92

Tate, F. 85
teacher education 9; English and schooling in early 20th century 79–94; NSW 85
teacher training 90
teachers 9, 73, 84–8, 92, 93; competence 89; early 1900s 101; identity 80, 94; New Education 84; pupil 83–4; qualified 90; quality 8; secondary school 91; South Australia 81; sympathetic 92
Teacher's Journal, The 60, 63

teaching: in Australia 80; English 88–9
Teaching of history and civics in Victorian secondary schools (Hoy) 62
technical schooling 24
temporality 6
Terman, L. 30
testing 21; mental 39; psychometric 45
tests: intelligence 29, 38; psychological 41
Thomas, J.: and Meredyth, D. 58
Tindale, N. 69
Trade and Commerce Committee 84
training: vocational 28
training college methods 87
Turner, I.S. 85, 86, 89, 91; and McRae, C.R. 85, 86
Turner, J.: and Knibbs, G. 83, 86
Turning Points (Carnegie Council, 1989) 19
12–15 problem 21, 22, 26–7, 30
12–15 specialist treatment 22
Tyler, D.: and Johnson, L. 5

United Kingdom (UK) 99; New Education Fellowship (NEF) 59, *see also* Britain
United States of America (USA) 36, 38, 67
universal schooling 31
utopianism 3–4

Victoria 29, 42, 47–8; Education Department 47–8; educational guidance scheme 43–4; history 61; record cards 43; school systems 18; schooling 18; Vocational and Child Guidance Centre 45, 47, 48
Victorian Teachers' Union (VTU) 57, 59
vocational guidance 7, 40, 40–6, 50, 51

Webb, D. 4
Western Mail 47
White Australia Policy 94
White, C.: and Openshaw, R. 100
Whitehead, C. 101–2
Williams, A. 18, 24, 85
Williams, F.E. 69
working class 22
world-mindedness 62
Worry Clinic 45
Wrenn, C.G. 36
Wright, K. 7, 35–52, 102, 104; and McLeod, J. 1–10
Wyndham, H. 44

young people 106

Zilliacus, L. 66, 67